BELIEFS AND IDEOLOGY

KENNETH THOMPSON, B.A., D.Phil.
Reader in Sociology
The Open University, Milton Keynes

ELLIS HORWOOD LIMITED
Publishers · Chichester

First published in 1986 by
ELLIS HORWOOD LIMITED
Market Cross House, Cooper Street,
Chichester, Sussex, PO19 1EB, England
and
TAVISTOCK PUBLICATIONS LIMITED
11 New Fetter Lane, London EC4 4EE

Published in the USA by
TAVISTOCK PUBLICATIONS
and ELLIS HORWOOD LIMITED
in association with METHUEN INC.
733 Third Avenue, New York, NY 10017

© 1986 K. Thompson/Ellis Horwood Limited

British Library Cataloguing in Publication Data
Thompson, Kenneth, *1937–*
Beliefs and ideology.
1. Ideology   2. Sociology
I. Title
306   HM24

ISBN 0–85312–858–8 (Ellis Horwood Limited — Library Edn.)
ISBN 0–85312–859–6 (Ellis Horwood Limited — Student Edn.)

Phototypeset in Times by Ellis Horwood Limited
Printed in Great Britain by R.J. Acford, Chichester

Contents

Kenneth Thompson is Reader in Sociology at The Open University, and a noted authority on Emile Durkheim and the sociology of belief and ideology. His previous publications include *Emile Durkheim*, *Religion and Ideology* (with R. J. Bocock), and *Sartre* (with M. Thompson).

Editor's Foreword

The intellectual division between those perspectives which focus on belief and belief systems, and those which focus on ideologies, has been a longstanding feature of modern sociological analysis. The former have conventionally been crystallized in a recognizable specialism — the sociology of religion — whilst the latter has resided in Marxist theory (and thus in frequent opposition to 'bourgeois' sociology) or has been hived off into the relativist backwaters of the sociology of knowledge.

This opposition has its root, of course, in the conflict and competition between the perspectives of conservative and radical political philosphies. Marx's definitions of religion as 'opiate of the masses' seemed completely at odds with Durkheim's notion of religion as a representation of society, for example, when each is seen as derived from revolutionary or reactionary societal models. As Kenneth Thompson observes, such apparent divides become even more unbridgeable when Durkheim is presented as a functionalist sociologist of religion, and Marx as a 'vulgar' economist for whom culture is a mere reflex superstructure of an all-determining economic base.

Such divisions obscure the very real synergy between the Marxist exploration of the concept of ideology (especially when freed of the dismal task of Marxian exegesis) and conventional sociology of religion. It is more than simply misleading to allot the concept of ideology to a primarily political sphere and to treat belief systems as prototypically religious. Such barriers to enlightenment as are found in the sterile distinction between Marxism and sociology are naturally replicated in the apparent distinction between ideology and belief system. Although this distinction is more revealing of institutional boundaries than it is of fundamental differences of approach, there have been remarkably few attempts to promote the paradigm-switch which would break down the obstacles to a wider understanding. Georges Gurvitch attempted such a rapprochement a generation ago without notable success, and it is perhaps fitting that it is Kenneth Thompson, Gurvitch's principal translator, who now proposes a most imaginative unification of Durkheimian and Marxist thinking.

The most obvious effects of the divisions outlined above were the separation of questions about ideology and belief systems into two sorts. The first looked at religion and culture as contributors to the integration of society — treating belief systems as social 'cement'. This was the approach taken by most sociology of religion — although such notable treatises as Weber's Protestant Ethic thesis take a more questioning line. Contrasted with them was the more radical perspective which sees beliefs and ideologies as elements — even central components — of systems of social control. There is more than a whiff of critical rationalism in this latter approach, and it recalls the Young Hegelian origins of much of Marx's writings on religion and ideology. Their objective was the debunking of religious belief as a system of thought, in the service of a more general critique of the political order. The view of religion as the quintessential ideology — or system of distorted knowledge — was persuasive to political movements whose objectives were to overthrow both material and spiritual manifestations of the status quo. However, this view was at odds with, more sociological insight into the integrative functions of ideologies and belief systems, and in particular their roles in the affirmation of local, ethnic and even class identities.

Much of the field covered by both sociology of religion and the Marxist study of ideologies, was hitherto taken also to be the proper domain of the sociology of knowledge — a specialism with many authors but almost no institutional presence. Like the ideas with which it dealt, the specialism had no recognizable social base. Yet the concepts and theories of its chief practitioners — Scheler, Mannheim, Gurvitch, Merton, Lukacs, the critical theorists — have had an incalculable impact on both Marxist theory and sociology. What they have encouraged is an eclecticism that bridges the Marxism–sociology gulf, by putting questions about culture and ideology at the head of the agenda for a number of other spheres of sociology and social theory.

It is not perhaps going too far to suggest that Kenneth Thompson's book exemplifies this contemporary trend to take a more eclectic approach to questions about culture, ideology, belief and religion. I would also like to suggest that Thompson's openness to the insights of a number of apparently competing perspectives is not eclecticism for its own sake, but a welcome sign of new thinking, appropriate to the new social conditions which are so rapidly emerging in contemporary society. Much as new information technologies are dissolving organizational and institutional boundaries in so many domains, new social scientific thought has to be evolved to comprehend the forms of social stratification, of ideology, and systems of belief, which a post-industrial society generates.

Peter Hamilton

Acknowledgements

I have been greatly helped in the preparation of this book by discussions with colleagues associated with the Open University course on 'Beliefs and Ideologies', particularly Stuart Hall, Bob Bocock, James Donald, Veronica Beechey, Greg McLennan and Nick Abercrombie (although none of them should be held responsible for what follows!).

1

Theoretical Approaches

INTRODUCTION

The arguments in this book are partly intended as a response to the intellectual challenge presented to the sociology of belief by recent Marxist discussions of ideology. Some of the general theoretical aspects of that challenge have been summarized in the Open University course books on 'Beliefs and Ideologies' (1985), and by Nicholas Abercrombie in his *Class, Structure and Knowledge* (1980), and in Abercrombie *et al., The Dominant Ideology Thesis* (1980), and, more specifically with regard to the challenge to the sociology of religion, by Bryan S. Turner in his *Religion and Social Theory* (1983) [1]. In responding to these challenges, which are extremely wide-ranging, I will not attempt to cover all the various debates that have ensued, but rather confine myself mainly to those most relevant to topics which I have engaged with in my own works on the response of organized religion to social change, the sociology of knowledge and false consciousness, class cultures and the persistence of elites, control and ideology in organizations, folklore and popular culture, and the treatment of beliefs and ideology in the classical tradition of sociology (especially the influence of Durkheim) [2]. The intention of the book is to debate some of the key issues relating to the formation and social functions of beliefs and ideologies. Some of the debate will cover issues that were traditionally considered to be the province of the sociology of religion: religion as social cement, as an instrument of social control, and in its relations with other cultural phenomena or dimensions of social life. However, we will also pursue the arguments beyond the confines of the sociology of religion and suggest that the subject of beliefs and ideology deserves to be discussed in a broader framework (as it was in the seminal works of Marx, Weber and Durkheim). In this respect we will seek to answer the challenge of those critics, such as Turner, who have accused the contemporary sociology of religion of failing to engage with the major theoretical debates about ideology, French structuralist discussions of subjectivity and power, and critical theory's discussion of knowledge, the state and legitimacy. Consequently, in addition to broadening the list of topics to be discussed to include some references to beliefs and ideologies concerning work, the nation state, and youth sub-culture styles, we will also extend the sources of theoretical influence to include such figures as Althusser, Gramsci, Foucault, Habermas, and other contemporary theorists whose ideas have featured prominently in debates about beliefs and ideology but are seldom referred to in the more narrowly based sociology of religion. This book is about more than religion, therefore, but it gives religious beliefs and ideologies a prominent place and takes them as an initial focus or as a way in to more broadly based discussions of beliefs and ideology.

MARXISM AND THE SOCIOLOGY OF IDEOLOGICAL COMMUNITY

Religion provides a useful focal point or way in to the study of beliefs and ideology for a variety of reasons. It cannot be denied that it was used in that way by the early and classical sociologists, from Comte through to Durkheim and Weber, and even Marx developed his critique of ideology by starting first with the critiques of religion, which led him to comment that historically speaking, 'the criticism of religion is the prerequisite of all criticism' [3]. Goran Therborn, writing from a Marxist perspective about the classical tradition in sociology, maintains that the central sociological contribution to scientific discourse on society 'has essentially consisted in the discovery and study of the ideological community — i.e. community of values and norms — in human aggregates of various types and sizes' [4]. This is exemplified, as Therborn points out, by Durkheim, whose 'achievement in his early works was to delimit a theoretical space — the space explored by sociology. On the one side, it was bounded by the social substratum of moral and material density, the field of social morphology, on the other by the individual and his non-social urges and tendencies, studied by human physiology and individual psychology. Between those two poles there was an irreducible entity — the community of values, norms, and beliefs [5].

Although Therborn criticizes Durkheim and mainstream sociology for failing to allot a proper space to the determining effects of the forces and relations of production with respect to the ideological community (unlike Marxist historical materialism, which gives priority to that social determinant, and takes that as its object and the source of its problematic), he acknowledges that sociological analyses of the ideological community do have some genuine scientific merit. Unlike much of the purely negative criticism of sociology by earlier Marxists, which concentrated on exposing the ideological distortions of 'vulgar' sociology (just as sociologists dismissed vulgar Marxism), Therborn refreshingly insists on distinguishing between scientific and vulgar sociology, and advocates a Marxist critique of the former, not for the purpose of rejecting it, nor with a view to a synthesis, but to achieve a 'transcendance of sociology' and the development of historical materialism as *the* science of society. The aspiration to transcend the limitations of existing sociological theory is one that many sociologists share, but not all of them feel it necessary to assert that sociology and historical materialism are different social sciences with different objects of analysis, as Therborn claims. Furthermore, and more positively, there are grounds for believing that the sorts of discussions that are covered in this book give some support to the case for cross-fertilization between different theoretical frameworks with a view to mutual enrichment of the ensuing analyses. Certainly, the sociological analysis of ideological community can be enriched by the sort of Marxist critique advocated by Therborn:

> The ideological community refers to an external reality, to values and norms transmitted in empirical processes of socialization and determining men's social behaviour in ascertainable ways. We noted above that the object of sociology does not involve the assumption that society is a unitary ideological community: on the contrary, the discipline has explicitly dealt with relations of domination and conflict among groups, organizations and institutions governed by different values and norms . . . The tasks of a Marxist critique of sociology are . . . first to insert systems of values and norms into a historical totality, to articulate them with the forces and relations of production, with the state and with the class struggle based on these structures, and to demonstrate how the ideological community is determined by this totality. The second duty is to demonstrate how the ideological communities incarnated in different groups, organizations institutions and societies are structured by the class struggle, constituting different and mutable examples of the unity of opposites, contradictory unities of the values and norms of opposing classes (this would imply, for example, an analysis of organizations different from that of Max Weber, who perceived organizations of domination as expressions of the values and norms of the ruling class only). [6].

This statement indicates two of the main lessons that I hope to show the sociology of beliefs (or ideological communities) can learn from Marxist theories of ideology: firstly, the need to locate systems of beliefs and values within the specific social formation in which they articulate with the modes of production, the state, and class struggles; secondly, the need to investigate these ideological communities, which exist within specific organized collectivities (institutions, organizations, nation states, etc.), with an awareness that the apparent cultural unity of each of these masks the reality of past and present class struggles and contradictory values and norms. There is nothing intrinsic to sociology that need prevent it from giving full weight to these considerations in its models of society and its investigations of ideological communities. Indeed, I would maintain that the classical sociological model sketched out by Durkheim is quite capable of accommodating such considerations, even though it may not have given full weight to them in the way it was subsequently developed and used. (I have discussed Durkheim's model in my book *Emile Durkheim* in the 'Key Sociologists' series, and some of its aspects will be considered further in subsequent chapters.) The most important adaptation that has to be made to the model, in the light of Marxist materialist conception of ideology, is to the conception of the material or morphological level, where it needs to be recognized that the 'internal social dynamic is governed by forces and relations of production rather than by, say, demographic food/population ratios.' A second change of emphasis is that the idealist tendency of some sociologists, from Durkheim onwards, which caused them to attach over-riding significance to ideological interpellations of *what is good and right* (values), needs to give way to a greater consideration of interpellations of *what is* (cognition), and *what is possible* (imagination) [7].

Therborn's statements are significant because he has undertaken a careful consideration of the development of sociology and come to the conclusion that Marxism has a great deal to learn from the findings of sociology. Indeed, in the opinion of some sociologists, his own attempt to develop a new theory of ideology can be seen as an attempt to synthesize a sociological perspective with Marxism [8]. In view of his previous assertions that sociology and Marxist historical materialism have different objects of knowledge, it is doubtful whether he would agree that a synthesis is possible. However, leaving aside Therborn's own estimation of the possibilities for synthesis, we are free to reach our own conclusion as to whether there is anything intrinsic to sociology that need prevent it from assimilating theories, concepts and insights from Marxism. It is not my intention to enter into an epistemological debate about this because, as others have concluded, it is a well-trodden path that seems to lead nowhere [9]. The intention here is to explore and clarify the contribution that Marxist ideas (and those of others who would not call themselves Marxist, such as Foucault) can make to the sociology of beliefs and ideology.

DEFINITIONS AND TERMS

The most important contribution that recent Marxist debates can make to the sociology of beliefs and ideology is to give it a more socially and politically relevant focus. This is illustrated by Therborn's statement in *The Ideology of Power and the Power of Ideology* that his main concern is with the operation of ideology in the organization, maintenance and transformation of power in society. Another contribution lies in the rejuvenation and broadening of the concept of ideology so that it does not necessarily imply any particular content (falseness as opposed to scientific truth), nor does it assume that beliefs have attained a particular degree of coherence and elaboration. This approach rejects the narrow definition of ideology which restricts it to certain beliefs that are false or mystified (and so tied to the notion of 'false consciousness'), or to the narrow sense of certain sorts of intellectual doctrinal systems. In this way the concept is liberated from the confines of economistic Marxism, in the first instance and, secondly, from the clutches of political scientists and others who have restricted it to the doctrines of 'extremist' or sectarian groups and parties (a view illustrated by the 'End of Ideology' debate in the 1950s) [10]. According to Therborn, ideologies are social phenomena of a discursive kind, including both everyday notions and 'experience', and elaborate intellectual doctrines; both the 'consciousness' of social actors and the institutionalized thought-systems and discourses of a given society [11]. This is very close to the sociological definition of culture, as Abercrombie *et al.* have pointed out [12]. However, Therborn wishes to distinguish ideology from the 'almost all-inclusive notion of "culture" deployed in much British writing on working-class culture' and he defines culture as 'the ensemble of everyday activities and ideologies of a particular group or class, or as a more general inclusive concept for ideology, science and art and, possibly, other practices studied from the point of view of their production of meaning' [13]. Thus, despite the similarity of the broad concept of ideology and the sociological concept of culture, Therborn seeks to retain a specific analytical dimension in his definition of ideology. This analytical dimension includes the processes forgrounded in Althusser's attempt to give scientific precision to the Marxist theory of ideology: 'The operation of ideology in human life basically involves the constitution and patterning of how human beings live their lives as conscious, reflecting initiators of acts in a structured, meaningful world. Ideology operates as discourse, addressing or, as Althusser puts it, interpellating human beings as subjects' [14].

The basic characteristic of ideology, or the ideological element in cultural practices and discourses, according to this definition, is that it constructs subjects (or subjectivities). In the writings of Althusser and Therborn, these subjects are usually individual persons, but they could also be collective subjects, such as classes or corporate entities of various kinds. Ideology interpellates subjects in the sense that it addresses or hails individuals in a certain way, thereby bestowing a position and an identity on them. Therborn wishes to emphasize the dialectical character of all ideology as indicated by the opposite senses of the same word 'subject' in the expressions 'the subject of king X (or the social order Y)' and 'the subjects of history'. In the first sense 'subjects' refers to people who are subjugated under a particular force or order, whilst in the second sense it refers to the makers or creators of something [15]. Therborn refers to these two senses as 'subjection' and 'qualification' (by ideological interpellation individuals are qualified to take up roles, including the role of possible agents of change). The basic social functioning of subjection-qualification involves three fundamental modes of ideological interpellation. Ideologies subject and qualify subjects by telling them, relating them to, and making them recognize: what exists, what is good, and what is possible. One of the deficiencies of previous theories of ideology, as Therborn points out, is that they have often neglected one or more of these three interpellations. He cites the example of liberal theories of political ideology, including those concerned with 'consensus' and 'legitimation', which have often concentrated exclusively on the second mode of interpellation, shared values concerning the good society, form of government or regime, ignoring patterns of knowledge and ignorance, and of ambitions, hopes and fears. Similarly, the Marxist concern with class consciousness has focused on the first two aspects and neglected the third — a person can be a highly class-conscious member of an exploited class without seeing any concrete possibility of ending the exploitation.

I have taken Therborn's statements about ideology as an initial focus because he has made an effort to relate his own historical materialist approach to that of sociology and the analysis of ideological communities (even if it is mainly for the purpose of pointing out the differences), and because his approach incorporates some important Marxist contributions without tying itself down to what he calls 'Marxological exegesis'. However, as we will see, these contributions are most valuable with respect to the light they shed on the working of ideology through such processes as the construction of subjectivity and the relationship to structures of domination. They are also more open-minded than previously where it concerns questions of determination. Thus, in the case of Therborn's four historical materialist propositions about the determination of ideologies, the first two are very general and not specifically Marxist, and the other two, which are more characteristically Marxist, concerning class-relatedness and class-determination, he puts forward as nothing more than guides to research or fruitful hypotheses 'whose explanatory power will remain an open question in any given empirical study':

Proposition One: All ideologies exist only in historical forms in historical degrees of salience and modes of articulation with other ideologies.

'Proposition Two: All ideologies operate in a material matrix of affirmations and sanctions, and this matrix determines their interrelationships.

Proposition Three: All ideologies (in class societies) exist in historical forms of articulation with different classes and class ideologies.

Proposition Four: The patterning of a given set of ideologies is (within class societies) overdetermined by class relations of strength and by the class struggle. [16]

The first two propositions about the historicity and the determining effect of the material matrix on ideologies are sufficiently general to be acceptable to most sociologists. Even that reputed founder of sociology, Auguste Comte, insisted that 'sociology adds to our other means of research that which I have called the *historical method*', and although he rejected materialist reductionist explanations, such as those which 'attempt, for instance, to explain all sociological facts by the influence of climate and race', he believed that the strength of the 'positivist' sociological method was that, 'it satisfies and reconciles all that is really tenable in the rival claims of both materialism and spirititualism; and, having done this, it discards them both [17]. Emile Durkheim went further in his recognition of the determining effects of material structures or morphological factors, by giving due recognition to forms of organization, which are materially grounded, and to material resources and instruments. As he put it, when reviewing Labriola's account of Marxist historical materialism:

We believe it is a fertile idea that social life should be explained not by the conception of those who participate in it, but by profound causes which escape consciousness; and we also think that these causes must principally be sought in the way in which associated individuals are grouped. [18]

Therborn admits when comparing Durkheim with Marx that 'both had a fundamentally materialist approach to the study of social ideas' and that 'in their explanatory models can even be found an apparently term-by-term correspondence between Marx and Durkheim' [19]. What Durkheim rejected was economic determinism: 'Just as it seems true to us that the causes of social phenomena must be sought outside individual representations, it seems to that same degree false that they can be reduced, in the final analysis, to the state of industrial technology, and that the economic factor is the mainspring of progress [20]. Therborn is right to point out that, whilst Durkheim emphasized the social base or milieu as the determining factor of social evolution, he avoided reductionism by always conceiving social reality in terms of several distinct and irreducible layers, and that in his later works he tended to emphasize the multiplicity of levels rather than the determinant milieu itself. Thus, for example, once collective representations have been formed on the basis of a particular social milieu, they become partially autonomous: 'New representations consequently . . . have as their immediate causes other collective representation, and not this or that feature of the social structure [21]. Although it is true that Engels was at pains to assert in his letters to Schmidt and Bloch in the 1890s that the notion of relative autonomy and the specific efficacy of systems of ideas is also underwritten by historical materialism, to Durkheim and many other critics it was the 'vulgar' Marxism of economic determinism that threatened to bring social science into disrepute. It has taken a long time for economic materialism to be superseded by a historical materialism that gives due attention to the relative autonomy and specific effectivity of the various levels of the social whole. As I hope to demonstrate, Durkheim's model of the multi-layered total social phenomenon, and other sociological conceptions of the social structures and cultural processes that make up these layers, have had more to offer in this respect. On the other hand, Marx and later Marxists have formulated a more precise and effective conception of the material social base which, because it is a conceptualization more adequate to the specific character of the capitalist mode of production based on a particular form of class relations, offers a better guide to locating ideologies in relation to the system of economic and political power in a given society. In terms of Therborn's second pair of propositions this means that all ideologies within a capitalist society will be found to articulate in various ways with different classes and class ideologies, and although they are not necessarily directly determined by class factors, the articulation is 'over-determined' by the constellation of class forces. Class over-determination, according to a conception drawn from Erik Olin Wright, means that different classes *select* different forms of non-class ideologies and that class constellations of force *limit* the possibilities of ideological interrelationships and of ideological change. Thus:

> Proposition Four implies, for instance, that if we want to explain the different relative positions of Catholicism and nationalism in contemporary France and Italy, we should look at how these ideologies have been linked with different classes, and at the outcome of the struggles between these classes. Nationalism became linked with the bourgeois revolution, as a revolutionary rallying-cry and weapon against the dynastic state and its principle of dynastic legitimacy. The Catholic Church and the Papacy, on the other hand, were historically closely allied with the dynastic state and its dominant social forces. Catholicism therefore became a banner of the counter-revolutionaries and their clienteles. The radical and victorious revolution of the French bourgeoisie and petty-bourgeoisie may then be seen to have led to the triumph of nationalism, whereas the weaker and more moderate bourgeois revolution in Italy would explain a much stronger Catholic legacy. The bourgeois and the petty-bourgeois classes on one hand, and the quasi-feudal classes on the other might be seen as having 'selected' nationalism and Catholicism, respectively, in a particular conjuncture (which then cancelled the reverse options), and their respective strengths and weaknesses as having posed 'limits' to supra-nationalist and secular ideologies. [22]

We will give further consideration to these issues in subsequent chapters, particularly with respect to nationalism in different periods in Britain and America. However, at this point it is important to note that Therborn agrees with the sociological view that 'Ideological conflicts and competition are (usually) not directly determined by class relations and the class struggle. They operate through specific forms of social organization and process [23]. Some of these relatively autonomous levels of forms of social organization and social processes have been more extensively studied by sociologists than by Marxists, and the analysis of ideology has much to gain from what has sometimes been dismissed as 'bourgeois sociology'. As one Marxist critic commented with regard to the contribution of Althusser and other Marxist theorists of ideology:

Knowing that ideologies are simple or complex significations generated in specific social relations and practical contexts is not of itself enough to enable us to do improved empirical analysis . . . [T]he latter requires us to focus on the conception of social practice and that means that, like voluntarist or bourgeois sociologies of meaning, Marxism needs to explicate a conception of the 'micro' level of social life. [24]

(The micro-sociology of Georges Gurvitch, to be discussed in Chapter 4, was developed partly because of his awareness of such a lack in Marxism.) Unfortunately, despite the value of Althusser's contribution in re-emphasizing the importance of ideology and his attempt to relate unconscious symbolic structures to the maintenance of power relations, he is still vulnerable to charges of class reductionism and economism. The danger exists of producing once again a theory of ideology that is mechanistic and functionalist. Ideology can appear to be simply a reflection of the economic structure that is transmitted into people's brains via seemingly private institutions which are really part of the state (these are the institutions Althusser refers to as Ideological State Apparatuses, e.g. the Church, the legal system, the Media, the Trade Unions, the Schools, and Political Parties) [25]. It is ironical that Althusser, whose position is regarded as standing in critical opposition to bourgeois sociology, should lay himself open to the same criticisms that have been levelled at Durkheim's sociology. In fact, it can be argued that Durkheim was less guilty of the faults of a mechanistic and functionalist view of the relations between ideology and social relations than Althusser [26]. His model allowed more relative autonomy and specificity to the various levels of social phenomena, and his view of the articulation of these levels and the causal flow between them has generated insights and analyses that should be regarded as complementary to those deriving from a historical materialist approach, rather then being dismissed as 'bourgeois' or 'idealist', as is often the case. Thus, in addition to drawing selectively on Althusser, Gramsci and other Marxist theorists of ideology, we will also look to sociology and anthropology for insights into the various layers and social dimensions outlined in Durkheim's model of the continuum of social phenomena, which can be summarized as follows.

I.   *Morphological or material substratum*
(a) Volume, distribution and density of population (including 'moral density', that is, the degree of interaction).

(b) Territorial organization. Material objects and resources incorporated in the society: raw materials, fuels, technological instruments (e.g. machinery), channels of communication, buildings, monuments, etc.

II. *Institutions (normative sphere)*
(a) Formal rules and norms — expressed in fixed legal and sub-legal formulae, moral precepts, religious dogmas, political and economic forms, occupational role definitions — or as expressed in determining language conventions and obligations of social categories.
(b) Informal rules and norms as applied in the preceding domains: customary models, collective habits and routines.

III. *Collective representations of a symbolic kind*
(a) Societal values, collective ideals; opinions; representations which the society has of itself; legends and myths; religious representations (symbols, etc.).
(b) Free currents of social life that are effervescent and not yet caught in a definite mould; creative collective thinking; values and representations in the process of emerging. [27]

Each layer of phenomena is crystallized to a different degree, and each exercises social constraint in some way, ranging from morphological factors that determine the availability of resources, to the constraining force of norms backed by sanctions, to the constraints imposed by language, the force of myths and symbols, and the pressure of public opinion. There is nothing very special or exhaustive about this checklist of different layers or levels of social phenomena. No doubt it could be differently arranged and supplemented. However, I would maintain that it is useful in reminding us of the full range of levels on which ideological processes can be found. Recent Marxist models of ideological processes have tended to concentrate on elements on one or more of the levels in Durkheim's model. The parallel is most evident, I will suggest, between Durkheim's model, as it relates to ideology and ideological community, and Althusser's theory of ideology in general. However, there are also parallels between Durkheim's layers of social phenomena (subsequently elaborated by Gurvitch into ten levels) and some of the phenomena outline by Gramsci (e.g. philosophical systems contrasted with the stratified deposits that make up the common-sense knowledge of the masses) and Foucault (e.g. an archaeology of knowledge uncovers layers of discourses and different regimes of truth). The point of these comparisons is not to try to make something out of a suggested superficial resemblance, but rather to indicate some of the lines of convergence that we will explore further.

SOCIOLOGY OF KNOWLEDGE/BELIEF AND THEORIES OF IDEOLOGY

It is sometimes suggested that the approaches of the sociology of knowledge/belief and of the Marxist perspectives on ideology are so different that there can be no fruitful exchanges between them. I have already indicated that there are grounds for doubting this, especially when we look behind the simple assertions of difference to see where the supposedly irreconcilable differences are to be found. Thus, in the case of Therborn's historical materialist propositions, the more general ones are perfectly reconcilable with a general sociological model of social collectivities, such as that deriving from Durkheim, and where the propositions are more specific with respect to determining factors, they are acceptable as fruitful sociological hypotheses. As we will see, there are extensive parallels between Althusser's theory of ideology in general and Durkheim's theory of religion. Similarly, there are parallels between Therborn's discussions of the ways in which different classes (or class fractions) *select* different forms of non-class ideologies, and Max Weber's account of *elective affinities* between different social strata and certain types of religious beliefs [28]. It is not the case that the *object* of analysis is completely different, but simply that there are different social theories about that object. The real problem, as Abercrombie has explained, is that whilst none of the concepts, ideology, knowledge, belief, are theory-neutral, ideology carries with it a large volume of theoretical baggage, in particular the notion of distortion. Nevertheless, 'Ideology is still a *form* of belief, even if one separately wishes to argue that its social causation has some impact on its validity' [29]. Furthermore, the notion of distortion as a defining characteristic of ideology has been rejected by Althusser and some other Marxists, who wish to depose the subjective consciousness as the origin of ideology construed as a distorted conception of reality, and more positively emphasize that the subject is determined in ideology which has itself a material existence. There is some question as to whether Althusser has really eliminated distortion as a defining characteristic of the Marxist concept of ideology, as he continues to speak of 'misrecognition' and 'imaginary relation' in order to distinguish it from science. Larrain argues that a Marxist definition of ideology must maintain the characteristic of distortion, but he distinguishes this from 'false consciousness'. Whereas Lukacs equated ideology with false consciousness, Larrain insists that falsity and distortion are not the same. Ideology has a basis in reality, but it is a distorting relationship because it is embedded in practices that are socially contradictory, and as a result of that embeddedness it cannot rise above the contradictions to render a true account of them [30]. Put in sociological terms, this would mean that to the extent that people are over-socialized into roles (including such general roles as worker, capitalist, consumer, etc.) and institutional practices, they are unlikely to be able to think differently and to be able to see the social contradictions (e.g. between ideals and practices, and between different goals). This sociological view of ideology need not be limited to the form in which it was adopted by Karl Mannheim, who advocated social criticism by supposedly detached intellectuals. There is no reason why it could not embrace Marxist diagnoses and remedies if they seem more convincing in specific instances. If, for instance, the fundamental contradictions in a capital social formation can be shown to derive from an inherent tendency of that mode of production to depend on the exploitation of one class by another, and ideology serves the function of distorting a perception of that exploitation, then sociological analysis should include a critique of that ideology. If sociology fails to do that, then it lapses into ideology — meriting the label of 'bourgeois sociology'. Similarly, if sociological analysis limits itself to disclosing other social contradictions, such as that between democratic principles and elite or bureaucratic domination, then it will still lapse into ideology through its dilution or displacement of the problematic of contradictions deriving from exploitative class relations in a capitalist mode of production. But there is nothing to stop the sociology of beliefs from exercising a constant vigilance against lapsing into ideological distortion. Some of the beliefs and rituals that it studies may not be directly determined by class relations and class struggle, but they can be examined in terms of their ideological effects and for their relationship to other discourses and discursive practices that are more directly class-related.

DURKHEIM, ALTHUSSER AND A THEORY OF IDEOLOGY IN GENERAL

Durkheim's theory of religion was based on the study of totemism in pre-industrial societies, but it was intended to have a wider applicability. In view of what has been said, it will provide an interesting test case of whether the sociology of beliefs inevitably lapses into ideology or is capable of assisting in the exposure and critique of ideology. At this stage we will confine ourselves to mentioning some of the positive contributions it has made to a general theory of ideology or ideological community, comparing it with that of Althusser, and leaving aside for the moment the requirements of a theory of particular ideologies in concrete social and historical formations. Both Durkheim and Althusser see ideology as a universal dimension of social life [31]. This universality derives from the socially cohesive function of ideology, which provides a mythical or imaginary representation of the underlying social structure/system of social relations. It is not just a matter of cognitive explanation of those relations, as both Durkheim and Althusser believe that this function will be increasingly taken over by social science to the detriment of ideology/religion. Rather, ideology serves the function of reproducing the social order by symbolically representing it as a unity in which the individual subject has a place, and at the same time the symbols operate to generate a sense of identification and commitment. Thus the individual is hailed or constructed as a subject within a symbolic discourse, and it is these symbolic discourses which constitute ideological or imaginary communities. The task of sociological analysis is to decode the system of symbolic representations (which are not free-floating, but embodied in material things and practices), and where possible reveal their referents in the order of social relations.

This broad outline of a general theory of ideology, viewed as a universal social dimension, is adequate as far as it goes. It sketches out the processes of symbolization and the imaginary as representations of the real conditions of existence — the underlying social relations into which individuals are inducted, and which exist independently of our will. However, when we turn from a theory of ideology in general to theories or analyses of particular ideologies, which are located in concrete social and historical formations, Althusser and Durkheim have less to offer. Their general theories need to be supplemented by some more detailed specification of the components and processes that enter into the formation, transmission and reception of ideologies. Here we will examine the key contributions made by other theorists, especially Gramsci, and the studies of a number of historians and sociologists. However, it is worth re-stating my main conclusion that a Durkheimian sociology of ideology (although he did not use the term *ideology* in this connection) is compatible with an Althusserian definition of ideology as systems of representation — composed of concepts, ideas, myths, or images — in which people live their imaginary relations to the real conditions of existence [32].

CULTURAL PROCESSES AND IDEOLOGICAL EFFECTS

It is arguable that there has been too much emphasis in the past on trying to define what ideology really is and too little attention given to exploring the various levels of social life on which cultural processes produce ideological effects. It is for this reason that I agree with Anthony Giddens in using the concept 'ideology' to refer to ideological aspects of social systems and not as a type of symbol-system (contrasted with science or as distorted knowledge). Any component of culture can be ideological. (However, we can still continue to speak of 'ideology' or 'an ideology', provided it is understood as elliptical: to treat a cultural complex as an ideology is to treat it as ideological) [33]. Most of the definitions of ideology are useful for what they affirm, because they direct attention to at least some of the levels or processes of culture that have particular ideological effects. But they are often unsatisfactory because of what they neglect (not because of what they *exclude*, as every definition must be exclusive). Thus, it is possible to agree with Althusser's definition, with its emphasis on imaginary representations which are nevertheless inscribed in material phenomena and lived out in everyday life. He also directs attention to some important ideological functions — the interpellation of subjects and social reproduction. But the concept of 'interpellation of subjects' has rather mechanical implications, suggesting that people automatically recognize themselves in terms of the categories by which they are 'hailed', and it neglects the processes by which people 'negotiate' their own identities and the variety of ways in which they are motivated to act in accordance with them. The possible rigidities of Althusser's approach have only been avoided by combining it with other perspectives, such as Gramsci's emphasis on struggle and contestation. Consequently, the tendency in this book will be to follow a policy of theoretical eclecticism, even at the risk of failing to achieve a strict conceptual consistency. Phenomenological approaches will be used to supplement more structuralist perspectives. Hence, Gurvitch's typologies of 'depth-levels' of culture, and his phenomenologically derived accounts of different forms of sociality, will be drawn on to supplement more structuralist conceptions, such as those of Althusser and Barthes. Similarly, both 'culturalist' and 'structuralist' perspectives on popular culture or everyday-life culture will be adopted at various points, in so far as they seem useful in generating insights on a specific issue. On the whole, we will emphasize the positive contributions that these various approaches have to offer, and not their weaknesses. This strategy need not be taken as sanctioning a 'cavalier' attitude towards the logical differences between different philosophical and methodological approaches. However, as with the arguments about whether sociology and Marxist historical materialism are fundamentally irreconcilable, insistence on differences can degenerate into internecine strife or sterility. In the immediate post-Second World War period there were few sociologists equipped and willing to grapple with such seemingly opposed approaches as historical materialism, phenomenology and Weberian social action theory, Durkheimian sociology, and the emerging structuralist methods. Georges Gurvitch was ahead of his time in this respect, and although his efforts at synthesis may have been premature and so ultimately a failure, he anticipated many of the components of more successful recent syntheses, such as that of Anthony Giddens, who echoes Gurvitch in his sympathetic critique of historical materialism and in examining time-space variables in relation to power in the theory of structuration [34]. These, and other open-minded efforts at theoretical synthesis, such as those of Stuart Hall and his collaborators in studies of ideology, have provided fresh insights that have yet to be exploited in fields such as the sociology of knowledge and beliefs (including the more narrowly defined sociology of religion) [35].

REFERENCES

[1] Cf. Robert Bocock and Kenneth Thompson (eds.), *Religion and Ideology*, Manchester, Manchester University Press, 1985; James Donald and Stuart Hall (eds.), *Politics and Ideology*, Milton Keynes, Open University Press, 1985; Veronica Beechey and James Donald (eds.), *Subjectivity and Social Relations*, Milton Keynes, Open University Press, 1985; Nicholas Abercrombie, *Class, Structure and Knowledge*, Oxford, Blackwell, 1980; N. Abercrombie, S. Hill and B. S. Turner, *The Dominant Ideology Thesis*, London, Allen & Unwin, 1980; Bryan S. Turner, *Religion and Social Theory*, London, Heinemann, 1983.

[2] Cf. Kenneth A. Thompson, 'Bureaucracy and the Church', in D. Martin (ed.), *A Sociological Yearbook of Religion 1*, London, SCM Press, 1968, pp. 32–46; *Bureaucracy and Church Reform: The Organizational Response of the Church of England to Social Change, 1800–1965*, Oxford, The Clarendon Press, 1970; 'Introductory Essay' in Georges Gurvitch, *The Social Frameworks of Knowledge*, trans. by M. A. and K. A. Thompson, Oxford, Blackwell, and New York, Harper Torchbooks, 1971; 'Introductory Essay' in Joseph Gabel, *False Consciousness*, trans by M. A. and K. A. Thompson, Oxford, Blackwell, 1975; 'Church of England Bishops as an Elite', in A. Giddens and P. Stanworth (eds.), *Elites and Power in British Society*, Cambridge, Cambridge University Press, 1974; (with G. Salaman), 'Class Culture and the Persistence of an Elite: The Case of Army Officer Selection', *Sociological Review*, **26**, 2, May 1978, pp. 283–304; 'The Organizational Society' and 'Organizations as Constructors of Social Reality', chs. 1 and 10 in G. Salaman and K. Thompson (eds.), *Control and Ideology in Organizations*, Milton Keynes, Open University Press, 1980; 'Religious Organizations' in J. McKinlay (ed.), *Processing People: Cases in Organizational Behaviour*, London and New York, Holt, Rinehart & Winston, 1975, pp. 1–40; 'Religious Organizations: The cultural perspective', in G. Salaman and K. Thompson (eds.), *People and Organizations*, London, Longman, 1973, pp. 293–302; *Auguste Comte: The Foundation*

of Sociology, London, Nelson, and New York, Wiley, 1975; *Emile Durkheim,* London, Tavistock and Ellis Horwood, New York, Methuen, 1982; 'Introduction' to Kenneth Thompson (ed.), *Readings from Emile Durkheim,* London, Tavistock and Ellis Horwood, New York, Methuen, 1985; 'Religion, Class and Control' in R. Bocock and K. Thompson (eds.), *Religion and Ideology,* op cit., pp. 126–153.

[3] Karl Marx, *Contribution to the Critique of Hegel's Philosophy of Right,* London, Penguin, 1975, p. 243.

[4] Goran Therborn, *Science, Class and Society,* London, New Left Books, 1976, and Verso edn. 1980, p. 224.

[5] Ibid., p. 258.

[6] Ibid., pp. 428–429.

[7] Goran Therborn, *The Ideology of Power and the Power of Ideology,* London, New Left Books, 1980, p. 18.

[8] Nicholas Abercrombie, Stephen Hill and Bryan S. Turner, 'Determinacy and Indeterminacy in the Theory of Ideology', *New Left Review,* **142,** Nov.–Dec. 1983, 55–66, p. 56.

[9] N. Abercrombie, 1980, op. cit., p. 168.

[10] The chief proponents of this view were Daniel Bell, Seymour Lipset and Edward Shils. Cf. C. Waxman, *The End of Ideology Debate,* New York, Funk & Wagnall, 1968.

[11] Therborn, *The Ideology of Power and the Power of Ideology,* op. cit., p. 2.

[12] Abercrombie *et al.,* 1983, op. cit. p. 56.

[13] Therborn, *The Ideology of Power . . .,* p. 6.

[14] Ibid., p. 15.

[15] Ibid., pp. 16–17.

[16] Ibid., pp. 32–40.

[17] Auguste Comte, *Cours de philosophie positive,* 1830–42, quoted in K. Thompson, *Auguste Comte,* op. cit., pp. 75 and 78.

[18] E. Durkheim, 'Review of Antonio Labriola, *Essays on the Materialist Conception of History',* in Thompson, 1985, p. 36.

[19] Therborn, *Science, Class and Society,* p. 251.

[20] Durkheim, 'Review of Antonio Labriola', in Thompson, 1985, p. 29.

[21] Durkheim, 'Representations individuelles et representations collectives', in his *Sociologie et Philosophie,* Paris, 1951, p. 43, and quoted in Therborn, 1976, p. 255.

[22] Therborn, 1980, pp. 38–40.

[23] Ibid., p. 39.

[24] Colin Sumner, *Reading Ideologies,* London and New York, Academic Press, 1979, p. 208.

[25] Louis Althusser, 'Ideology and Ideological State Apparatuses', in

Lenin and Philosophy and Other Essays, London, New Left Books, 1971.

[26] Cf., for a comparison of functionalist and mechanistic elements in the theories of Durkheim and Althusser, S. Strawbridge, 'Althusser's Theory of Ideology and Durkheim's Account of Religion: An examination of some striking parallels', in *Sociological Review,* **30**, 1, 1982, pp. 125–140; Colin Sumner, 1979, p. 28. For a critique of Althusser for defining ideology on the same ground as Durkheim's general sociological model, see J. Rancière, 'On the Theory of Ideology', in *Radical Philosophy,* **7**, 1978, pp. 2–10.

[27] Thompson, 1982, p. 60.

[28] Cf. Max Weber, *The Sociology of Religion,* London, Methuen, 1963. For a comparison of Weberian and Marxist approaches to the sociology of religious sectarian movements, see the articles by Bryan R. Wilson, 'A Typology of Sects', and Stuart Hall, 'Religious Ideologies and Social Movements in Jamaica', in Bocock and Thompson, 1985, op. cit., pp. 297–312 and 269–96.

[29] Abercrombie, 1980, p. 167.

[30] Jorge Larrain, 'On the Character of Ideology: Marx and the Present Debate in Britain', in *Theory, Culture and Society,* **1**, 1, 1982, 5–22, p. 15.

[31] This discussion develops suggestions drawn from Strawbridge, op. cit., and Bernard Lacroix, *'The Elementary Forms of Religious Life* as a Reflection on Power (*Objet Pouvoir*)', in *Critique of Anthropology,* **4**, 13–14, 1979, pp. 87–103.

[32] The justifications for the various terms in this definition, especially the term '*real* conditions of existence', are well argued by Stuart Hall, 'Signification, Representation, Ideology: Althusser and the Post-Structuralist Debates', in *Critical Studies in Mass Communication,* **2**, 2, June 1985, pp. 91–114. Durkheim does examine specific ideologies in relation to real conditions of existence in his only major historical work, *The Evolution of Educational Thought,* trans. P. Collins, London, Routledge & Kegan Paul, 1977; see the discussion in my *Emile Durkheim,* 1982, op. cit., pp. 160–165.

[33] Anthony Giddens, *Central Problems in Social Theory,* London, Macmillan, 1979, p. 188.

[34] Cf. Anthony Giddens, *A Contemporary Critique of Historical Materialism,* London, Macmillan, 1981, and Kenneth Thompson, 'Introductory Essay' in Georges Gurvitch, *The Social Frameworks of Knowledge,* op. cit., pp. ix–xxxvi. The relation of ideology to perceptions of time and space, particularly with respect to blocked and

reified conceptions, is discussed in my 'Introductory Essay' to Joseph Gabel, *False Consciousness,* op. cit.

[35] Cf. Stuart Hall's publications listed above, and those mentioned in subsequent chapters.

2

Social Cement

SOCIAL CEMENT AND SOCIAL CONTROL

There are a number of theories of religion as ideology which seem to draw on the notion of it acting as some kind of 'social cement' — binding together disparate elements in a social formation. Gramsci, using the example of the Catholic Church to illustrate a hegemonic cultural order, says that it preserves 'the ideological unity of the entire social bloc which that ideology serves to cement and unify' [1]. His view of it was in terms of a dynamic process of struggle in which the dominant class tried to assert a cultural leadership. Some versions see it as a surface phenomenon, less a process of 'cementing' and more a matter of 'plastering' over the underlying cracks in the social fabric and hiding them from view; this is the 'masking function' interpretation. Another view locates the cement at a deeper level, tracing social integration to the binding nature of fundamental shared beliefs. The first view is exemplified in certain statements of Marx and Engels, such as Engels's *Introduction to Socialism: Utopian and Scientific,* where English religiosity in the nineteenth century was contrasted with working class radicalism and bourgeois free-thinking on the Continent and explained in terms of the greater cunning of the English bourgeoisie in safeguarding their class interests by spreading religion among the workers and pretending to be religious themselves. This is only one of several different accounts of the ideological functioning of religion that Marx and Engels gave, but it is the one in which they place most emphasis on social control being maintained by active manipulation of religious ideology. They were also aware of the other side of the picture, which was that the workers were not just passive receivers of the ideology, but were active users of it in so far as it could serve as an expression of their real suffering and of their hopes for deliverance. Engels, in the passage referred to, goes on to argue that traditional religion, as the sedimented residue of philosophies that corresponded to past social relations, could not long continue under changed circumstances to have idological effects sufficient to 'prop up a tottering society'. And if traditional religion could not be relied upon for long, neither could the new sectarian version of the religion, such as the Salvation Army, 'which revives the propaganda of early Christianity, appeals to the poor as the elect, fights capitalism in a religious way, and thus fosters an element of early Christian class antagonism, which one day may become troublesome to the well-to-do people who now find the ready money for it' [2]. By viewing religious ideas and other ideologies as sites of contestation and weapons in the class struggle, Marx and Engels recognized that the view of religion as 'social cement' was only half the picture: it might be true of traditional religion, and the attempt of the ruling class to use it for the purpose of social control, but it did not account for the fact that changes in social relations undermined its effectiveness, and that religious ideas could be used to contest domination. We will return to these issues of religion as a means of social control and as a resource for contesting such control and domination (see Chapter 3). Firstly, however, I would like to examine some applications of other 'social cement' theories which attribute social integration or social reproduction to the effect of ideological integration or domination at the level of basic social values, or at other levels of the discourses and practices in the cultural complex that constitutes an 'ideological community'. The main theoretical approaches that will be drawn on are Durkheimian sociology and Althusserian Marxism, whilst bearing in mind that these different schools or streams are internally very varied and have developed well beyond the ideas of their founders.

DURKHEIM AND IDEOLOGY

There are different views about which aspects of Durkheim's theoretical legacy have subsequently been most influential and relevant to the analysis of ideology. To some extent these views reflect judgements about whether to place more emphasis on Durkheimian functionalism, such as that developed by Talcott Parsons, or Durkheimian structuralism, as it was developed by Lévi-Strauss and other structuralists [3]. Durkheimian functionalism as it relates to ideology suggests that the routinized features of society express motivational commitments that people have internalized through socialization — norms that govern behaviour are an expression of shared values and beliefs (a collective conscience or consciousness). Structuralism, by contrast, is a method that entails delving below the surface phenomena of social life to discover underlying relations whereby it is ordered, in a similar way to that in which combinatory elements are uncovered in linguistics (Lévi-Strauss drew on the linguistic theories of Saussure, Trubetskoy and Jakobson).

Both streams have developed useful Durkheimian insights concerning aspects of ideology. Functionalism has generated studies of boundary-maintenance through which ideological communities preserve their unity by defining deviance from normative behaviour and mobilizing negative sanctions against such deviant behaviour. (The study of the Salem witch trials by Kai Erikson provides a good illustration of this, as we will see) [4]. Structuralism has developed Durkheim's ideas on social classification whithin symbolic codes, as in the work of Mary Douglas on purity and pollution, and has extended the idea of decoding to all kinds of symbolic representation, giving rise to a science of semiotics or semiology as exemplified in the studies of Roland Barthes [5]. And although Althusser has rejected the label of structuralism for his approach, there are parallels between Durkheim's discussion of how religious representations function to position people and to give them an identity and Althusser's demonstration that 'all ideology has the function (which defines it) of constituting concrete individuals as subjects' [6]. It could be illuminating to keep these parallels in mind when examining some of the attempts that have been made to develop Durkheim's insights with reference to particular ideological processes in concrete social formations. For example, an understanding of the significance for the analysis of ideology of neo-Durkheimian studies of 'civil religion' would be enriched by an awareness that what is being studied is the construction of subjects through the articulation of several chains of discourses, each structured by a play of differences. This would provide a theoretical linkage to the related neo-Durkheimian explanations of why there is a greater religiosity in America than in England, which have been couched in terms of the ethnic diversity and religious pluralism of America, and the tendency of third-generation Americans to identify with different ethno-religious groups. This American neo-Durkheimian approach tends to be blended with a voluntaristic view which puts the emphasis on individuals choosing or deciding which identity to adopt, and ideological effects are regarded as unintended consequences of such purposive action. Such an approach contrasts with the structuralist emphasis of Durkheim and Althusser, according to which individuals are given their identities, or are constructed as subjects, by the discourses into which they are recruited or hailed. But this need not lead to a mechanical view of people being incorporated into a dominant ideology or common culture of shared values; the Althusserian view of ideology is more complex than that, picturing the ideological dimension as systems of representation in which men and women *live* their imaginary relations to their real conditions of existence ('real' in the sense that they exist apart from, or are not encompassed by, their ideological representation). The advantage of Althusser's formulation is that it does not fall into the oversimplifying trap of suggesting that there has to be a single dominant ideology to ensure social reproduction, as it has been accused of doing by the critics of a so-called 'dominant ideology thesis' (Abercrombie *et al., The Dominant Ideology Thesis*). As Stuart Hall points out:

> Note that Althusser says 'systems', not 'system'. The important thing about systems of representation is that they are not singular. There are numbers of them in any social formation. They are plural. Ideologies do not operate through single ideas, they operate in discursive chains, in clusters, in semantic fields, in discursive formations. As you enter an ideological field and pick out any one nodal representation or idea, you immediately trigger off a whole chain of connotative associations. Ideological representations connote — summon — one another. So a variety of different ideological systems or logics are available in any social formation. The notion of *the* dominant ideology and *the* subordinated ideology is an inadequate way of representing the complex interplay of different ideological discourses and formations in any modern developed society. Nor is the terrain of ideology constituted as a field of mutually exclusive and internally self-sustaining discursive chains. They contest one another, often drawing on a common, shared repertoire of concepts, rearticulating and disarticulating them within different systems of difference or equivalence. [7]

In view of this potentiality for focusing on the pluralism and contestative character of the discursive chains that make up an ideological terrain, it is unfortunate that Althusser's discussions of religion and ideology have largely been confined to the experience of French society (and perhaps other Latin countries) where there was a single dominant religious institution, the Roman Catholic Church. The consequence has been that his analyses show no awareness of the complications produced by religious pluralism within the field of ideological discourses. By contrast, neo-Durkheimian sociologists of religion have begun to give more attention to the processes by which religious discourses function to differentiate identities, such as on ethnic-religious community lines (e.g. Catholic, Protestant and Jew) which are then rearticulated within other systems of difference to constitute a higher level ideological community (e.g. American civil religion counterposed against the alien 'Other' of godless communism). The ideological effect of such processes with regard to social contradictions and power/domination, is that other divisions and constraints are 'masked' and the status quo is legitimated. Althusser's theory of ideology in general is similar to Durkheim's in its indication of the possibilities for such imaginary representations of social relations, and the construction of ideological communities into which subjects are interpellated. Both Althusser and Durkheim failed to develop their general theories in the direction of a detailed specification of types of particular ideologies in concrete social formations. (Max Weber's sociology of religion is much richer in this respect). Althusserians have not focused much attention on variations between societies with the same mode of production, whereas Durkheimian sociologists have been more inclined to pursue such comparisons and contrasts. The discussions about 'civil religion' in Britain and America provide a good example of this, as they illustrate that the particular articulation of chains of discourses varies significantly between societies and over relatively short periods of time.

FROM THEORY OF IDEOLOGY IN GENERAL TO THEORIES OF PARTICULAR IDEOLOGIES

Althusser distinguished his theory of ideology in general from a theory of particular ideologies, the latter referring to ideologies in concrete social and historical formations. Durkheim too was concerned with developing a theory of religion in general, hence his concentration on the 'elementary forms' of religion, and consequently he left himself open to the criticism that he neglected to study the specific structural factors that affected religion or ideology in the capitalist societies of his own time. In fact, both Durkheim and Althusser seem to have developed their general theories of religion and ideology on the basis of an implicit contrast between modern France (taken as representative of all industrial capitalist societies) and pre-industrial or pre-capitalist societies. In both cases their accounts of the changing position of religion on the ideological terrain suffered from a failure to consider specific variations between the ideological complexes in different capitalist societies. For example, neither considered the significance of religious pluralism for the production of ideological community in America, which was very different from that of France. (It is worth noting that Max Weber, in contrast with the two French theorists, focused more on particular ideologies and was suspicious of theories of ideology in general, and as a result was much more alert to the significance of American religious pluralism.)

Any analysis of the articulation of different discursive chains that constitute a particular ideological complex, such as that of America in a specific period, would have to consider the relations between religious discourses and those of ethnicity, politics and economics. As we will see, there already exists some material that could be used for such an analysis, and it has been produced by various neo-Durkheimian sociologists of religion who have carried out studies of religious denominationalism, ethnicity, and civil religion, in different periods. The next step in developing theories of particular ideologies in concrete social formations has to be based on a comparative analysis of the articulation of discourses in different societies and in different periods. A small step in this direction can be taken by comparing the situation of religion in relation to other ideological discourses in America with the equivalent complex of discourses in England, particularly with respect to 'civil religion' in the two societies. In the case of America we will examine the articulation of discourses such as religious sectarianism, ethnicity, nationalism and anti-communism. In the English case, the relations to be discussed are those between religion (especially the Church of England), nationalism and anti-revolutionary sentiment, royalty and imperialism. The comparison of the two cases should serve to illustrate the variable and dynamic nature of the articulation of discourses within a particular ideological field or complex. It may well also lead to the conclusion that there are certain outer limits to such variability which are set by the common economic characteristic of these societies — the fact that they are both based on a capitalist mode of production, entailing certain fundamental conflicts of class interests. However, theories of particular ideologies in concrete social formations have to address themselves to the variations as well as the shared characteristics. It cannot be assumed that there is an automatic and mechanistic relationship between mode of production, class interests, and ideology, such that there is always a dominant ideology. Nor can we depend on a functionalist theory which explains ideology as an automatic response to the needs of a social system, so that a common culture or set of values is bound to exist by definition: for Parsonian functionalism there is an assumed homology between social system and cultural system, just as in economistic Marxism the cultural superstructure must correspond to the economic base.

RELIGION AND IDEOLOGICAL COMMUNITY IN AMERICA

The first social fact that has to be considered with respect to the religious representations (beliefs and practices) that constitute religious discourse in America is that of diversity. In the complex relationships between religious practice and belief and other elements of culture and social structure, the extent of religious differentiation plays an important part. The Roman Catholic Church, for example, has followed a different path when it has been the sole or dominant religion, as in France, than that taken when it was only one among several or many. But the fact of religious diversity itself has far-reaching consequences that ramify throughout the social order. Religious diversity in the United States is a familiar and often noted fact. The 1936 Census of Religious Bodies, the only such official census ever undertaken in America, listed more than 250 different sects and denominations. A more recent estimate found 1187 distinct denominations, sects and cults, even though the majority of people gave their primary religious allegiance to about two dozen mainstream religious organizations [8]. The sources of the diversity are complex and include such factors as the variety of immigrant groups, the absence of a state religion, differences between settled areas and an open frontier, elements of democratic ideology that resisted religious as well as political authoritarianism, and a succession of charismatic religious leaders who managed to win over large areas or sections of population, such as Joseph Smith of the Mormons and Mary Baker Eddy of the Christian Scientists. One of the consequences of the diversity, it has been suggested, is that there has been a more continuous history of religious tolerance in America than in most other Western societies.

However, as with the history of all ideological complexes, the relations between sets of religious representations and communities, and between religious discourses and other discourses, has not been free of contestation and struggle. The American tolerance of religious diversity is far from being unlimited. Public opinion and the law have reacted against religious beliefs when they seemed to threaten to upset an existing balance of ideological forces. The tension cannot be attributed to the unorthodox nature of the theological beliefs in themselves, but has arisen over supposed threats to key elements of ideological community at the national level. Tension decreases when the threat disappears or becomes manageable due to changes in the sect's position or when there is change in the relevant secular discourses. Sometimes the threat diminishes because national uncertainties that were causing the sect to be seen as a threat themselves diminish. Examples of sects which have aroused fierce opposition at times because they clashed with other discourses or discursive practices and so seemed to threaten crucial values are: the Mormons, who threatened the monogamous family tradition; the Jehovah's Witnesses, whose loyalty was called into question and were perceived as a threat to national security because they refused to salute the flag and pledge allegiance; the I Am Movement, which was thought to exploit and defraud the aged; and the Black Muslims, who called into question the claimed non-racist nature of American society.

Periods of national tension due to perceived external threats or uncertainties can also affect the level of tolerance of religious diversity (or ideological deviance). The confrontation with the Jehovah's Witnesses reached a climax in the period of tension leading up to America's entry in the Second World War, and it ebbed when the nation became more ideologically unified after Pearl Harbour. As one sociologist commented after examining the case: it seems surprising to us now that there should have been a widespread fear that American civilization was threatened by a handful of Jehovah's Witnesses' children refusing to salute the national flag at school, but that was the finding of the Supreme Court in 1940 [9]. The Court's opinion was that:

> National unity is the basis of national security . . . The ultimate foundation of a free society is the binding tie of cohesive sentiment. Such a sentiment is fostered by all those agencies of the mind and spirit which may serve to gather up the traditions of a people, transmit them from generation to generation, and thereby create that continuity of a treasured common life which constitutes a civilization. 'We live by symbols'. The flag is the symbol of our national unity, transcending all internal differences, however large, within the framework of the Constitution. (Minersville School District v Gobbitis, 1940.) [10]

There could not have been a better statement of Durkheim's view of the part played by symbols and rituals in maintaining a traditional form of social solidarity ('mechanical solidarity'), and of the function of punishment of deviants in order to reaffirm solidarity. Such a process was obviously at work in this case, as was indicated by the large number of attacks on Jehovah's Witnesses after the announcement of the Court's ruling. In Nebraska a Witness was lured from his house and castrated; in other towns Witnesses were mobbed; and in Richwood, West Virginia, the chief of police and the deputy sheriff forced a group of Witnesses to drink large doses of castor oil and paraded them through the streets, tied together with police department rope. And yet, three years later, the Court reversed itself and ruled that children could not be barred from public schools for refusing to salute the flag. (West Virginia State Board of Education v Barnette, 1943) [11]. Several reasons have been suggested for the change of attitude, but Pfeffer established that the main sociological factor was probably a resurgence of national ideological community after Pearl Harbour, and a new fear that the threat to security came from Japanese Americans, rather than the relatively insignificant Jehovah's Witnesses.

The discourses that construct American society as a field of social differences are organized around several categories, some of which are concerned with internal societal differences and others with a difference that rests on a contrast with an external Other (e.g. Orientalism as incarnated in the Japanese threat, or atheistic communism as represented by the Soviet threat). A change in the relations with the external Other, whether or not it is a change of focus or intensity, will have repercussions on the articulation of the internal social differences. Hence, after the Second World War, when there was a change of focus towards a revived fear of communism, this now constituted the boundary limit to American tolerance of internal ideological diversity. Communism had always been regarded as incompatible with the ideology of free enterprise capitalism, but the ascendance of Soviet Russia to the position of the perceived external threat to national security intensified the search for deviants on the Left. The McCarthy witch-hunts for communist subversives after the Korean War in the 1950s have been interpreted by neo-Durkheimian sociologists as a ritual reaffirmation of the nation's faltering identity and as a way of revitalizing itself after a collective crisis [12]. Religious discourse was again playing a prominent part in articulating the difference that cemented America as an ideological community: the contrast was drawn between the atheistic nature of communism and the religious basis of America's national identity. It is not surprising that sociologists in the 1960s began to talk about an 'over-all American religion' and a 'Civil religion' that furnished Americans with their basic identity, or interpellated them as religious subjects, as Althusser might say.

A crucial set of articulations in the American ideological complex has been between the discourses of ethnicity and religion, on one level, and, at the 'higher' level, between the discourses of religion and nationalism, which overlap or fuse together (they connote or summon up one another), united by their common opposition to godless communism. Of relevance to an analysis of the first level is Herberg's study *Protestant, Catholic, Jew* (1960). Herberg affirmed that American immigrant groups, by the third generation, had lost their ethnic-based identities as they went through the 'Melting Pot' of assimilation and that they then identified with one of three religious communities — Protestant, Catholic or Jew. The religious community helped the individual in a complex society to answer the question of 'who am I?'; in Althusser's terms, it interpellated them as subjects through a re-articulation of the discourses of ethnicity and religion. Owing to the social psychological leanings of American sociology at that time, Herberg's thesis tended to be interpreted as an explanation of individuals' solutions to their need for sociability or a sense of belonging. However, it can be interpreted in terms of the articulation of discourses — religion, ethnicity, nationalism — and an articulation of partial and total ideological communities. Herberg's thesis portrayed religion as attaching people to different primary communities, but in a way that was non-divisive because there were no fundamental ideological differences between the three religious communities. They were 'three diverse, but . . . equally American expressions of an over-all American religion, standing for essentially the same "moral ideals" and "spiritual values"' [13]. What Herberg labelled as 'the American Way of Life' included a positive evaluation of religion itself, a faith in the democratic system, a belief in progress, and a sense of national mission.

There have been many criticisms of Herberg's thesis, both with respect to its generalization about a long-term trend away from ethnic community towards attachment to a broader religious community, and with respect to its neglect of class factors. On the first issue, he failed to take account of the periodic nature of the perceived external threat which, in the 1950s, reached panic proportions and intensified pressure to conform to a common 'Americanism'. In the 1960s there was a greater concentration on perceived internal differences and a resurgence of ethnic consciousness, particularly among blacks. Even with respect to the 1950s, the position of blacks presented a glaring exception to the generalization about integration into three religiously based ideological communties. Lenski's *The Religious Factor* (1963) reported on data from a 1958 survey of the Detroit area and provided quantitative evidence that seemed to show there were at least four important religious-ideological communities: White Protestants, Black Protestants, Catholics and Jews. Lenski found consistent differences between these groups on matters such as work values, political preferences, attitudes towards saving and spending, social issues, family size and family ties, educational achievement and social mobility. There even seemed to be support for the continuing salience of Max Weber's thesis in *The Protestant Ethic and the Spirit of Capitalism* that Protestants achieved higher occupational status than Catholics because their religious beliefs gave them a stronger motivation to achievement. However, the results of a study published in 1971, which sought to replicate Lenski's survey in the same area, failed to reproduce the same results [14]. It is likely that what social differences there had been between Catholics and Protestants as ideological communities in the 1950s had begun to decline in the next decade. Lenski himself admitted that this might be the case, and so cast doubt on the Herberg thesis that religious community allegiance had increased in importance as a source of self-identity and integration into American society. A summary of the many studies into the question of whether membership of the different religious communities correlated with different levels of socio-economic achievement concluded that religious affiliation did not explain much of the variance [15]. However, when religion closely articulated with ethnicity (common ancestry) to form ethno-religious communities then there were significant differences still. Such differences over basic world view were particularly marked between different Catholic ethnic groups, such as Italian and Irish [16]. No doubt the differences are even greater for more recent immigrant Catholic ethnic groups, such as Hispanics (more than three-quarters of Spanish-speaking Americans are Catholics). Surveys by the National Opinion Research Center (NORC) have found that ethnic sub-cultural differences are greater than denominational differences with regard to what they called 'fundamental world view' [17].

This discussion of American functionalist sociology's attempt to developing a convincing theory of ideological community is not intended to be a comprehensive critique. If it were such, then we would spend more time pointing out the significant absence of the factor of class and class conflict in the theory, and the absence of any discussion of the part played by ideology in securing the legitimation of relations of domination. There have been many such critiques of what is left out by this theory, and of its assumptions. We are more interested here in discovering what can be learned from it that is of use in developing a theory of a particular ideology in a concrete social formation, especially with respect to the articulation of discourses and levels of ideological community. However, it must be said that, in retrospect, Herberg and the functionalist sociologists of the 1950s and early 1960s do seem to have been remarkably complacent in their assumption that the articulation of ideological discourses at various levels proceeded smoothly like a well-oiled machine or a process of organic evolution. The Melting Pot thesis and functionalist sociology shared in an optimistic ideology according to which groups of diverse backgrounds and cultures were being assimilated into a social system, whilst variety was still preserved and tolerated (the thesis of pluralism). This optimistic ideological resolution of contradictions appears to have been achieved by stringing together a chain of linked propositions:

(1) Assimilation and pluralism were both possible because, according to Herberg, 'the American system is one of stable co-existence of three equi-legitimate religious communities' [18].
(2) The co-existence of three communities was functional for the social system because it enabled people to locate themselves and to find an identity, and this sense of continuity and roots was particularly important for the later generations who had little attachement to the ethnic culture of their immigrant ancestors.
(3) These broad religious communities provided a cultural and associational link between the individual and the national society.
(4) This created no ideological conflict because the three religious communities were expressions of an over-all American religion.

The theme of an over-all American religion was symptomatic of the functionalist adaptation of Durkheim's sociology. It emphasized the contribution of religion to the integration of social systems, and it equated social system with the nation state. Durkheim had contrasted the 'mechanical solidarity' of simpler societies, based on the like-mindedness of members who shared common religious values, with the 'organic solidarity' of complex societies, which was based on the complementarity of the different roles performed by members. But this organic solidarity in its pure form had to be based on a spontaneous division of labour, whereas in fact it tended to be based to a large degree on a forced division of labour, under which people undertook tasks and occupied positions not by virtue of a truly free choice but because of unequal power relations. In Durkheim's view, spontaneous attachment to norms (as distinct from coerced attachment deriving from an imposed discipline) could only occur when the forced division of labour was mitigated [19]. The functionalist theorists of religion in American society preferred to stress Durkheim's discussion of ritual as a process by which society reaffirmed itself periodically, and they seized on a passage to this effect at the end of *The Elementary Forms of the Religious Life*. But Durkheim went on to say that such ceremonials were not likely to be very successful in contemporary society and that it was hard to see what would replace them in the way that in the cognitive system science was replacing religion.

The functionalist interpretation of the American social system being integrated as an ideological community by an over-all American religion seemed most plausible in the 1950s and early 1960s. A typical application of this theory was William Lloyd Warner's *Family of God: A Symbolic Study of Christian Life in America* (1961), which developed the thesis of his earlier book *American Life: Dream and Reality* (1953) [20]. Warner gave particular emphasis to the function of national rituals in reaffirming the nation's sacred unity, such as Memorial Day rites, when the honoured dead 'become powerful sacred symbols which organize, direct, and constantly revive the collective ideals of the community and the nation [21]. The theme was taken up by Herberg, as we have seen, and then elaborated in a succession of works by Bellah, who defined this American *civil religion* as a 'set of religious beliefs, symbols and rituals growing out of the American historical experience interpreted in the dimension of transcendence' [22]. America's historical experience was interpreted by the civil religion in terms of myths drawn from the common Jewish and Christian heritage, such as the imaginary representations of being a 'chosen people' living in the 'Promised Land'. In Althusser's terms, the religious ideology constituted concrete individuals as subjects by subjecting them to God, the

'Unique Absolute Other Subject', who had called them, and so they were united in their common calling. This religious discourse was also closely articulated with existing political and economic discourses. It celebrated the American Way of Life, which included such elements as the Constitution, in the region of politics, and free enterprise in economics. The civil religion 'sacralized' and gave ideological significance to key events and ceremonies in these related secular regions of social life: Memorial Day, the birthdays of Washington and Lincoln, the Fourth of July, Veterans Day, and Thanksgiving. These were given an importance that purely religious festivals had in societies with an established or state religion. The secular saints were figures such as Washington and Lincoln, and the sacred shrines could be visited at Arlington and Gettysburg. Also, the civil religion was most prominent in its ceremonial form at Presidential Inaugurations, when the authority of the state received its sacred legitimation.

In the 1960s internal divisions and conflicts began to loom larger than the unifying effects of an external ideological threat. Indeed, the divisions of opinion over the Vietnam War reflected the doubts as to whether communism posed as great a threat to American ideals as did internal inequalities of power and wealth. Black militancy increased and gave birth to religious manifestations like the Black Muslims, who rejected many elements of the civil religion. The Vietnam War provoked widespread questioning of America's sense of superiority and mission. Many young Americans left the country, rejecting the ideology which hailed them as chosen people in a promised land. Furthermore, criticism of the ideology itself arose and sociologists attributed some of the social problems and the Vietnam War to tendencies within American civil religion [23]. Another view was that the civil religion also provided ideological resources for those who opposed the American involvement in Vietnam, which echoes the point made by Volosinov about the 'multiaccentuality of the ideological sign', that there is always scope for struggle over the meanings of signs and symbols [24]. It was argued that the civil religion does not sanctify the society as it exists and as an end in itself, but rather opens up the possibility of bringing the nation under a higher law against which it can be judged. Even within the parameters of a functionalist version of Durkheim's theory of religion, it was possible to make the case that the sacred symbol system referred to an ideal version of the society.

The internal divisions and ideological disputes of the late 1960s and early 1970s provoked the development of a neo-Durkheimian theory of religion that was much more conflict-oriented. Whereas in the earlier decade the discussion had centred on presidential inaugurations and national holidays as ritualistic mechanism for renewing common moral sentiments, the new focus was on scapegoating and witch-hunts as ritualistic mechanisms which created deviants and so served to produce a sense of solidarity in periods of tension. The concept used to identify such processes was that of *boundary crisis*. The concept was introduced in Kai Erikson's study of the seventeenth-century Salem witch-hunts, and it was subsequently applied to events as diverse as the Chinese Cultural Revolution and the Watergate Crisis [25]. Erikson's notion of a boundary crisis was inspired by Durkheim's discussion of the function served by crime in reproducing communal solidarity. In punishing crime, which offended the collective conscience, the society's ritualistic venting of its wrath re-affirmed the moral order. Erikson argued that a society need not wait for someone to go outside its moral boundaries, but at times could achieve the same effect by moving its moral boundaries and so create deviants. He reasoned that communities would manufacture deviants in this way when their collective existence was threatened from outside. In this way they could then ritually re-affirm the threatened, blurred, weakened, or insecure community. His example was taken from the seventeenth century Massachusetts Bay colony and the three 'crime waves' it experienced, the most famous of which was that concerning the Salem witch-hunts. The interesting feature of Erikson's neo-Durkheimian explanation is that it provides a useful example of the articulation and re-articulation of a religious discourse with legal, political and economic discourses, particularly with respect to property rights. He traces the genesis of the witch-hunts to the political and economic uncertainties after the British king revoked the charter of the Massachusetts Bay colony and the settlers began to fear for its future and for their titles to property. In 1676 King Charles II 'began to review the claims of other persons to lands within the jurisdiction of Massachusetts' and in the colony itself 'the courts were picking their way through a maze of land disputes and personal feuds, a complicated tangle of litigations and suits'. Something like open party bickering had broken out, and a visitor to Boston in 1668 observed that the people were 'savagely factious' in their relations with one another and acted more out of jealousy and greed than any sense of religious purpose [26]. The religious discourse provided reasons for the colony's troubles, as manifested in the many sermons, prior to the witch-hunts, which were on the theme that the settlers must expect God to turn His wrath on them because the colony had lost its original fervour and sense of mission, and there was the threat that they would have to return to the wilderness, which was peopled with devils. The elements of popular religion and superstition in that discourse supplied a scapegoat which was also functional for strengthening ideological community: persecution of imagined witches as deviants helped to re-affirm the common identity and moral boundaries of the community.

More recently, a similar neo-Durkheimian functionalist explanation has been used to account for the course taken by the Watergate crisis: 'The system needed rites of moral solidarity after the divisive Vietnam War and used Nixon's violations of normal political conduct as the basis for a revitalization campaign'.

The result of this moral drama, which was played out at length in front of a national television audience, was that,

> The *system* America as a set of collective arrangements, as a functioning corporate order, *worked*. America lived up to its ideals, overcame threats to the Republic, and reaffirmed the fundamental beliefs and assumptions upon which it was founded. Watergate was one of the best examples of the reaffirmation of collective sentiments and common beliefs in modern societies that we have seen for a long while. [27]

Although this type of explanation has been described as Durkheimian and functionalist, because of its emphasis on beliefs and social practices that reaffirm social solidarity, it is also a 'social cement' theory of religion as ideology, in some respects compatible with Althusser's definition of ideology as systems of representation — composed of concepts, ideas, myths, or images — in which people live their imaginary relations to the real conditions of existence. Where it has been developed as a theory of a particular ideology in a concrete social formation, as in the explanation of outbreaks of scapegoating and witch-hunts, it has usually included some reference to underlying conflicts and social contradictions, which are masked or misrecognized. Although Althusser is somewhat equivocal about the significance of the misrecognition or distorting effects of ideology, it is an essential characteristic in Marx's view of religion as ideology, and it is implicit in Durkheim's theory of religion [28].

RELIGION, NATIONALISM AND IDEOLOGY

Despite their attention to underlying social conflicts in relation to ideologies such as civil religion and those associated with boundary maintenance of an ideological community whose unity is threatened, these neo-Durkheimian theories still suffer from two weaknesses. Firstly, they neglected issues of power and domination, especially with respect to social class relations. Secondly, the functionalist mode of explanation still took the form of suggesting that things happened because the system 'needed' them to happen. Some critics would say that both these tendencies are to be found in *The Elementary Forms of the Religious Life,* although a closer reading of that work suggests that neither tendency is inevitable or unqualified [29]. Similarly, although critics like Larrain and Hirst have suggested that Durkheim did not have a sociologically viable theory of ideology, I believe it is possible to find the elements of such a theory in his study of religion, even though that study was mainly concerned with classless societies [30]. Following on some suggestions by Bernard Lacroix about *The Elementary Forms of the Religious Life* being an analysis of power, I believe it is possible to construct a Durkheimian theory of ideology, and that for this purpose we should give more attention to the structuralist style of analysis of the operation of religion, rather than to the functionalist causal explanation. The first point to note in this respect is that, as Lacroix puts it, for Durkheim:

> In the last analysis, religious beliefs are only a presentation which society makes of itself to itself: a crude image and hence a parody, a foreign presentation in which the object is hardly recognizable and, in short, a re-presentation. [31]

Durkheim provides a detailed analysis of the process by which social relations are lived in an imaginary form through ideological representations, such as religious beliefs. As collective representations, the religious beliefs carry and bestow authority because they seem to emanate from a transcendent source — they transcend the individual, sectional interests, utilitarian or mundane concerns; they have a 'halo of disinterestedness', as Benedict Anderson says of the ties that bind us to the nation as an imagined community [32]. Durkheim also provides examples of the coding procedures by which these systems of representation are constructed in the form of discursive chains that articulate differences and unity. In the case of the totemic religion of the clan-based societies of the Australian aborigines, sometimes the collective representations are arranged in terms of differences that accord with a binary logic of opposition, such as sacred v. profane; others are unitary like the clan totem. These categories and their logic are socially constraining, they set rules of thought and behaviour which have the power to elicit obedience. However, the social conditions or relations that gave rise to them are no longer evident, the effect of their origins is not directly decodable; 'the process of refraction therefore functions irreparably according to a logic of misrepresentation' [33].

For much of the time the 'misrepresentation' or 'misrecognition' aspect of systems of collective representation is not of great significance for the functioning of social systems. The shared categories and rules are inscribed in routine practicies and customs that are accepted without question. Hence there is some truth in the comment by the authors of *The Dominant Ideology Thesis* to the effect that the compliance of working class people is based on dull conformity to established practices and routines, rather than because their consent has been won by incorporation into a dominant ideology or set of normative beliefs. However, where ideology does become important is in situations or periods where there is heightened uncertainty, strain or crisis in social relations. At such times the previously less contested ideological community becomes more contested (there is never a complete absence of contestation over meanings, if only because the relation between signs and what they signify is a 'slippery' one). It is then that the aspect of 'misrepresentation' and 'misrecognition' is of greater significance and may even serve a crucial function in cementing over the cracks in the social fabric. The logic of differences then has to be re-articulated, as was evident in the civil religion ideology of America in the 1950s, with reference to godless communism, and in the various cases of witch-hunting and scapegoating.

One of the most important ways in which 'misrepresentation' or 'misrecognition' occurs is in bestowing an aura of 'naturalness' or a halo of 'disinterestedness' on the social relations which they represent. Sometimes the 'naturalism' includes a reference to God's divine will, as in the nationalist appeal of American civil religion. (At other times the State, which is not exactly the same as the imagined community of the nation, claims a legitimacy for its actions by reference to a 'disinterested' technical-instrumental logic that also rests in the natural order of things) [34]. In his essay 'Ideology and Ideological State Apparatuses' (1971), Althusser attempts to put ideology back into orthodox Marxist theory, with a greater degree of relative autonomy than ideology was previously allowed when it was regarded as a simple superstructural reflection of the economic infrastructure. He does this in the first instance via a theory of the state, rather than in terms of the social constitution and effects of complexes of discourses and practices. He does eventually place ideology within specific sets of discourses and practices, but his discussion is still couched in terms of ideology as produced by the state fulfilling the functions demanded by the economic structure. His basic argument is that the analysis of ideology must be conducted from the standpoint of seeing how ideology reproduces the relations of production; it is simply an aspect of the reproduction process:

. . . the reproduction of labour power requires not only a reproduction of skills, but also, at the same time, a reproduction of its submission to the rules of the established order, i.e. a reproduction of submission to the ruling ideology for the workers, and a reproduction of the ability to manipulate the ruling ideology correctly for the agents of exploitation and repression, so that they, too, will provide for the domination of the ruling class 'in words'. [35]

Althusser says that Ideological State Apparatuses (ISAs), which appear as 'private' institutions, such as the Church, Law, Media, Trades Unions, Schools, Political Parties, are part of the public state because they function for the state in reproducing ruling class power, and they are called ideological because they function primarily through ideology. It is debatable whether it is advisable to tie the discussion of ideology so closely to a theory of the state and the reproduction of relations of production. Perhaps because of this slant, Althusser downgrades the contemporary ideological significance of religion (which he equates with *the* Church, reflecting an assumption about the typicality of the French situation and the position of the Roman Catholic Church), and says that the crucial ideological institution is now education. There is some truth in this when it is offered as a comment on the contrast between the relative importance of these institutions in feudalism and late capitalism. However, it becomes a misleading generalization if applied across the board to all contemporary capitalist societies. It is more productive to concentrate on the actual articulation of different discourses or institutions in concrete social formations (America, Britain, France, etc. in particular periods). Education no doubt does contribute more directly to the reproduction of relations of production, but religion may still be a potent factor in combination with other discourses in the construction of ideological communities, such as the imagined community of the nation.

It can be argued that a more central reference of ideology in late capitalist societies is to the nationalist element in the nation–state couplet. Some legitimation of state authority may accrue from nationalist ideology, but it is the nation that wins allegiance rather than the state, which is frequently derided and devalued by current conservative ideologies. There is pride in being British or American, but the demands of the state are resisted within the ideology. Of course, this is a misrecognition of the social relations that are represented by the appeal of nationalism; the nation is an imagined community, whilst the state is a real condensation of power that requires subjects and subjection. In most cases when a nationalism wins adherents the state consolidates its domination over its subjects, except in those cases where there are competing nationalisms within the state, such as Scottish or Welsh nationalism. And behind the ideological rhetoric that is critical of the state, its domination is often being strengthened by building up what Althusser calls the repressive state apparatus — the armed forces, the police, and its general surveillance and intelligence agencies. Furthermore, the same ideological complex that down-plays the state and exalts the nation is often intertwined with religious revitalization campaigns that favour 'old time religion' (which usually means uncritical acceptance of the authority of the Bible or dogma) and traditional (e.g. Victorian) values. It is no coincidence that the ideological complexes of capitalist societies in the recent period of economic slump and political conservatism have included fundamentalist and Evangelical religious movements, which articulate with their political equivalents through movements such as those of the so-called 'Moral Majority' in America. In the 1980s the terms 'Reaganism' and 'Thatcherism' have been labels for broad ideological complexes that span a wide range of articulated discourses, including politics, economics, religion and familialism.

The authors of *The Dominant Ideology Thesis* may have been right to criticize Althusserian Marxist theorists of ideology, and the Parsonian functionalist theorists of common culture, for over-stressing the incorporation of people into a community of shared values as a prerequisite for the reproduction of the relations of production or the maintenance of social order in late capitalism. However, the editor of the series in which that book appeared, Tom Bottomore, was right to point out in his introduction that we must be careful not to throw out the baby with the bathwater. He suggests that, whilst there may not be a cohesive 'dominant ideology' which recruits subjects among the subordinate classes and so positively subjects them to the domination of a ruling class, the ideologies of nationalism and individual achievement may inhibit and confuse the development of the counter ideology of a subordinate class. However, this still makes it sound as if the terrain of ideology is populated by unitary class ideologies, expressions of the experience and interests of a dominant class or a subordinate class. It is more fruitful to think of the ideological terrain as a complex of discourses which have ideological effects, and the balance of forces in that field as being always in flux and the site of contestation over meanings. The complex of discourses recruits people as subjects and constructs ideological communities. The nation is one such ideological community and it is certainly the case that, the more it occupies the consciousness of people and attracts their allegiance, the less likely they are to give their allegiance to competing ideological communities, such as revolutionary movements in which a consciousness of shared class interests predominates. It is for this reason that the most successful revolutionary movements have been those which have managed to combine their appeal with that of nationalism, as in anti-colonial movements.

It is not surprising that nationalism and the nation attract the greatest allegiance in the modern world, much more so than other ideological communities acting alone, such as those based on sets of 'doctrines' (which used to be regarded as the epitome of ideology) — socialism, fascism, capitalism, Catholicism, Protestantism, or even Islam. (It is an Islamic Iran that attracted widespread support in that country, not pure Islamic ideology stripped of national embodiment; similarly with respect to Zionism.) Furthermore, as Benedict Anderson is careful to point out, it is not that nationalism somehow supersedes religion, but that 'nationalism has to be understood, by aligning it not with self-consciously held political ideologies, but with the large cultural systems that preceded it, out of which — as well as against which — it came into being' [36]. The two relevant cultural systems were religious community (e.g. Islam, Christianity, Buddhism) and the dynastic realm (e.g. the Habsburgs, Stuarts, Bourbons, etc.), which in their heyday were the taken-for-granted frames of reference that nationality is today.

Anderson defines the nation as 'an imagined political community — and imagined as both inherently limited and sovereign'. He adds that 'It is *imagined* because the members of even the smallest nation will never know most of their fellow-members, meet them, or even hear of them, yet in the minds of each lives the image of their communion' [37]. He quotes Gellner to the effect that 'Nationalism is not the awakening of nations to self-consciousness: it *invents* nations where they did not exist' [38]. The important point here is not the suggestion of 'falseness' but that nationalism rests on a particular type of imagining; as Anderson makes clear, all communities larger than those based on face-to-face contact (and perhaps even these) are imagined. In the case of nationalism, the community is limited and sovereign (it does not encompass the whole world and it demands the total allegiance of those people it does encompass), and it establishes a deep fraternity. The fraternity of nationalism is so deeply established that millions have been prepared to kill or die for it. With the pluralization of religions and the break-up of dynastic empires, the nation emerged as the ultimate ideological community for most people, the one with the strongest imagined sense of timelessness, disinterestedness and naturalness (the latter characteristic deriving from the effects of a national print-language, although this need not be confined to one nation, exclusive territory, and the sense of being born into that nationality or having been assimilated into it by 'naturalization').

Anderson asks the question whether nationalism is better viewed as an ideology — Nationalism-with-a-big-N, like 'liberalism' or 'fascism', or should it be regarded as belonging with 'kinship' and 'religion'? I agree with his judgement that it is better viewed from the latter perspective. But whereas Anderson does not spell out what he means by ideology in this context, I would want to insist that the concept 'ideology' should be thought of as referring to aspects of symbol systems (or systems of representation) and not to a type of symbol system (contrasted with science or valid knowledge). The key ideological aspects are those by which systems of representation interpellate people as subjects and construct imagined (ideological) communities, and that these have political significance in so far as they are determined by, or help to sustain, existing social relations of power, particularly within class-based societies. In analysing nationalism within a concrete social formation, such as America or Britain, these general ideological processes have to be translated into the particular forms in which they occur in each instance. This entails examining the articulation of the various discourses that support each other in producing the actual character of that specific imagined community — that nation. The descriptions of civil religion in America and Britain can be used for this purpose. They are particularly revealing with respect to the articulation of religious and political discourses in the construction of the imagined national community in each case.

NATIONALISM AND RELIGION IN BRITAIN

A variety of discourses and sets of differences have been articulated to construct the imagined community of the British nation at different times. Some of the most interesting are those in which religious and political discourses combined together to produce an ideologically unifying nationalism. In the period of internal upheaval and class conflict that accompanied the Industrial Revolution such a combination occurred in response to the perceived threat posed by revolutionary France. New politically conservative theories of the nation were developed by Burke, Coleridge and others, drawing on religious as well as political discourses. Public opinion was mobilized against the alien threat and British national characteristics were rediscovered or invented. Religious discourse was one of the key sites where there was a struggle to produce the required ideological effect of cementing national unity and rooting out any divisive tendencies. Nowhere was this more evident than in the remarkable change that took place in Methodism, which at one stage was regarded as something akin to a revolutionary fifth column, but which after the French Revolution became a pillar of support for King and country, and during the French wars passed resolutions to that effect at its annual conferences in 1794, 1797, 1798 and 1799 [39].

Methodism was suspected of revolutionary leanings because many of its religious practices were unconventional and dangerously democratic, it had called into question the hierarchical order of Church and state, and its evangelical enthusiasm seemed almost as much a threat to the established order as that of revolutionary enthusiasts. The older dissenting sects, such as Presbyterianism, Congregationalism and Unitarianism, had long been regarded as intellectually suspect with regard to patriotism. Throughout the eighteenth century there had been in dissenting ranks a drift away from their earlier position of support for the monarchy and constitution of 1689. Many of them had favoured the American cause during the war of independence, and they had strong ties with their co-religionists in the New World. One of the chief targets picked out by Edmund Burke and other theorists of the new nationalist doctrine was Dr. Richard Price's *A Discourse on the Love of our Country*, delivered on 4 November 1789 at the meeting-house in the Old Jewry, to the Society for Commemorating the Revolution in Great Britain. In his discourse, Price, who was a Unitarian minister, argued that love of country was a passion which, like other passions, must be regulated and directed. It should not degenerate into prejudice, blinding us to the merits of other countries and the faults of our own; patriotism could be a form of collective selfishness [40]. Although God had endowed us with partiality for kindred, neighbours and fellow-countrymen, such partial affections must be subordinated to universal benevolence. The anti-patriotic arguments of Price and others such as William Godwin in his *Political Justice* (1793), were characterized by three aspects: an insistence that loyalty to a nation should be proportioned to that nation's moral worth, a suspicion of human emotion, and a religious and political individualism that made the individual prior to and more fundamental than the community. By contrast, Burke's powerful anti-revolutionary and pro-nationalist treatise, *Reflections on the revolution in France* (1790), gave emotion preference over reason, declaring it more *natural*, and argued that a universal benevolence could only be approached by easy stages, building up from family and local attachments to the nation and perhaps eventually to mankind. Burke's theory emphasized cultural practices as the source of unity. A nation was a web of practices which instilled social and moral discipline, and an essential part of that discipline derived from an established Church, which consecrated the state and provided powerful incentives to obedience and order. William Coleridge developed this nationalist theory and the role of the Established Church even further than Burke. He argued against religious individualism and in favour of the national Church, and its *clerisy,* as the main agent of cultivation, 'to form and train up the people of the country to obedient, free, useful, organizable subjects, citizens, and patriots, living to the benefit of the state, and prepared to die for its defence [41]. The French wars may have caused hardship, but he thought they had made the nation more serious, moral and unified, and in 1834 he suggested that another threat of invasion might be good for morale [42]. (In recent years conservative ideologists have sometimes expressed a similar awareness of the morale-boosting effects of war and a yearning for a return to the unity of wartime Britain.)

These new political doctrines of nationalism drew on religious, philosophical and familial discourses to make their case, but they were also a response to an imagined threat, and their proponents showed an awareness of the benefits for ideological unity that followed from denouncing deviants and closing ranks against the external threat of the alien Other — revolutionary France. In these respects there are some parallels with the neo-Durkheimian social cement theories of civil religion and witch-hunts in America. There are also some parallels between the discussion of the nation by Burke and Coleridge, and recent Marxist theories of ideology as social cement. Like Louis Althusser a century later, the conservative theorist Burke had an awareness that ideology was inscribed in social practices. As one commentator on Burke's doctrine puts it:

> By implication, Burke has provided a powerful reply to cosmopolitans who object to nations as artificial and arbitrary; all human life is artificial and conventional, and each nation embodies a specific set of conventions. The nation as a system of practices is a distinctive mode of collective existence. [43]

Burke's *Reflections on the Revolution in France* provides a fascinating example of the re-articulation of existing political discourse and the redefinition of historical events in order to construct a new ideological community — in this case the conservative imagined nation, Britain. As Stuart Hall argues, it is no exaggeration to say that Burke 'high-jacked' the 'Glorious Revolution of 1688', snatching it from Whig/Liberal tradition, where it was associated with individual liberty and the overthrowing of the entrenched and arbitrary power of the monarchy and aristocracy. He appropriated or re-articulated this symbol of liberal triumph and used it to underpin a conservative view of English history and the constitution. The key concept that he used for this purpose was that represented by the word 'ancient'. He wrote that: 'The Revolution was made to preserve our *ancient* indisputable laws and liberties, and that *ancient* constitution of government which is our only security for law and liberty' [44]. This redefined '1688', so that it no longer was seen as having served to consolidate the break with the past brought about by the Civil War, but was now presented as preserving the ancient law, liberties and constitution. It was mythically represented as a continuity, not a historical break, and Burke fits it into a 'tradition' which he had constructed for himself, which stretched back in an unbroken chain of events to Magna Carta. Burke's political discourse also links up with the discourse and ideology of the family, referring to this tradition as a family inheritance, and with religious discourse:

> In this choice of inheritance we have given to our frame of polity the image of a relation in blood; binding up the constitution of our country with our dearest domestic ties; adopting our fundamental laws into the bosom of our family affections; keeping inseparable, and cherishing with the warmth of all their combined and mutually reflected charities, our state, our hearths, our sepulchres, and our altars. [45]

Burke was intent on inflecting the imagined community of the British nation in a particular political direction. It was a conservative direction because it sought to preserve an established social order and distribution of power, and it claimed a legitimacy and authority for that order on the basis of tradition. We have here a good example of the relationship between power and the imaginary representation of social relations which together have the effect that we have defined as ideology. In the case of nationalist discourse it 'invents' an imagined political community in a way that is ideologically effective; the real social relations that occur within the territory concerned are overlaid with a particular cultural meaning expressed in terms of an imaginary relation — that of being British in a conservatively defined sense.

It is worth recalling at this point Althusser's definition of an ideology from the essay in *For Marx*:

> Ideology is the expression of the relation between men and 'their' world, that is, the (over-determined) unity of the real relation and the imaginary relation between them and their real condition of existence. In ideology the real relation is inevitably invested in the imaginary relation, a relation that expresses a will . . . a hope, or a nostalgia, rather than describing a reality. [46]

This definition is very relevant to understanding what was at issue in the attempts to construct a British identity or ideological community in the period after the French Revolution, particularly with respect to the religious element. Althusser would not deny that people actually lived together within what was called the British Isles at that time, and that this was a 'real relation'. But it was 'lived' — experienced by those who lived there — within a set of meanings which were socially constructed and historically defined, and those meanings were being contested. There was contestation over the generation of the theories (as for example between rival theorists such as Price and Burke), over their transmission (such as the rivalry between the churches), and at their point of reception (in different regions and classes).

The transmission of an ideology of British identity depended to a large extent on the Church, but here there were problems because Christianity was divided and no church could claim a majority of the people in all parts of the British Isles. In fact, religion was one of the major sources of division with respect to national identity. As one ecclesiastical historian puts it:

> . . . modern British history, perhaps more than the history of any other European state, discloses a complex inter-relationship between political attitudes, ecclesiastical allegiances and cultural traditions. The Christian religion in the British Isles, in its divided condition, has in turn been deeply involved in the cultural and political divisions of modern Britain and Ireland. Churches have been, in some instances and at some periods, vehicles for the cultivation of a 'British' identity, corresponding to the political framework of Great Britain and Ireland. They have also been instrumental, in part at least, in perpetuating and recreating an English, Irish, Scottish or Welsh identity distinct from and perhaps in conflict with 'British' identity, both culturally and politically. [47]

Many of the strains and conflicts over social relations in the British Isles during the period we are discussing were manifested in the form of struggles over national identity and within religious discourses and institutions. The conservative political theorists often identified Britain with England and the consolidation of Britain entailed a process of 'Anglicization'. The result was that, although the Church of England failed to become the Established church for the whole of the British Isles (as many conservatives wanted it to be), the English language became the first language, even though there was constant opposition in some churches, such as in Wales. Along with the language went other cultural mores which were efficient for administration and commerce. The imagined political community of Britain grew out of, or to use Althusser's term, was 'over-determined' by the asymmetrical distribution of power in the structure of political and economic relations.

The importance of the Althusserian approach to ideology lies not so much in the distinction between 'imaginary' and 'real' relations — a distinction which has been disputed by critics such as Hindess and Hirst, but in the emphasis it gives to analysing how 'subjects' (whether individuals or collectivities such as nations) are culturally constituted. However, Althusser is less informative about the processes by which ideologies are generated, transmitted and received. This requires detailed comparisons of these processes with respect to particular ideologies in concrete social formations, which is why we are examining some examples of the interaction of religious and political discourses in America and Britain. There are clearly both similarities and contrasts between the two cases. Compared with France, for example, America and Britain have experienced more religious diversity. We have discussed some of the factors that gave rise to America's religious diversity, and we have noted that Britain had different established or majority churches in its constituent parts, such as the Presbyterian Church of Scotland, the Methodist Church in Wales, the Protestant churches in the north of Ireland, the Roman Catholic Church in southern Ireland, and the Church of England. This created problems for the transmission of a unifying ideology of national identity and community. In America the civil religion is not closely associated with institutional religion, but it does benefit from the high level of religiosity throughout the country. However, as befits a country in which church and state are officially separate, the main symbols and ritual events of the civil religion are concerned with the Presidency, national anniversaries, and sites where the heroic past is remembered. In Britain, the much lower degree of religiosity is balanced by the fact that the monarchy unites Church and state, so that ceremonies and celebrations involving royalty can combine the discourses of religion and politics to promote a sense of national community.

Some of the sharpest criticisms made by the authors of *The Dominant Ideology Thesis* were directed against members of the 'neo-Durkheimian ritualist school', such as Shils and Young and their famous article 'The Meaning of the Coronation' (1953). The critics interpret the neo-Durkheimians' argument as being to the effect that modern capitalist societies require a powerful collection of rituals in order to sustain a core of common values, into which the working-class had been successfully incorporated by the 1950s. Shils's view was that 'the coronation of Elizabeth II was the ceremonial occasion for the affirmation of the moral values by which the society lives. It was an act of national communion' [48]. This was certainly a common assumption shared by Talcott Parsons and other functionalist sociologists of the period. It was attacked at the time by Norman Birnbaum, who criticized Shils and Young for providing no evidence for the supposed value consensus in Britain, for treating Britain as a *gemeinschaft* form of society and for underestimating the political opposition expressed by the class-conscious working class [49]. The critique is extended by Abercrombie and his colleagues to cover later studies, such as that by Blumler *et al.* of the investiture of the Prince of Wales, where the ceremony was said to reaffirm values associated with family solidarity and national pride, and the study by Bocock of the ritual importance of various social gatherings and public events for the social integration of modern societies [50]. The problem with this critique is that it is too sweeping and it threatens to 'throw the baby out with the bathwater'.

There is a difference between a functionalist neo-Durkheimian theory which asserts that modern capitalist societies need rituals in order to incorporate the working-class into a core of common values, and a more structuralist neo-Durkheimian theory of ideology. The latter does not assume that a capitalist society is held together by incorporating the working-class into a common culture including a set of core values held by all members. Durkheim himself did not believe that a modern society could depend very much on *gemeinschaft* ties for its solidarity, although he left unspecified the degree to which civic rituals and ceremonies might continue to have a solidifying effect. He was conscious of the potency of national symbols, such as the flag, and Bastille Day celebrations. After all, these represented values and achievements that the nation could be proud of. However, the implication of his discussion is that modern society contains a variety of discourses and practices, economic, political, religious, etc., and that sociological analysis should be concerned with the ways in which they articulate with each other to promote or hinder different sorts of social solidarity. Some ties would be based on routine and custom, others on complementarity of functions and exchange of services, and there would be some that resulted from the awe and reverence that were inspired by symbols and ceremonies expressive of the experience of the transendence and power of the collectivity itself (both real and imagined social relations). Discourses and practices concerning royalty and religion can articulate together to produce a sense of awe and reverence for the imagined political community of the nation, just as international sporting events and wars heighten the sense of national differences. None of these can be taken as representing a core set of values that are essential for the reproduction of capitalist relations of production. But they are none the less important in constructing ideological communities and interpellating individuals as subjects.

Civic rituals, such as those which involve royalty, are dramatizations of the nation as a symbolic or imagined community. The king or queen is spoken of as head of the great family of the nation (or head of a family of nations in the case of the Commonwealth). Many of the civic rituals also celebrate points in the life cycle of members of the royal family, such as the marriage of Prince Charles and Lady Diana in 1981 and the annual celebration of the Queen's birthday. They frequently involve, and cement, a link with other institutions, as when the Queen as Head of State takes part in the State Opening of Parliament, or engages in the military ritual of the Trooping of the Colour on the monarch's official birthday. Not the least important function is the link forged with the nation's past by ceremonies such as that on Remembrance Day, when members of the royal family lay wreaths on the Cenotaph, and veterans of past wars are on parade. All of these events contain 'manufactured' or invented traditions, many of them of quite recent origin, which are broadcast to the nation, and members of the audience are drawn to identify with the imagined community and its past — in this way they are constituted and addressed as subjects [51]. The development of the coronation in Britain as a televised event is an apt illustration of the invention of tradition and of the manufactured nature of the process of communalization. The ceremony was adapted to the need of television, whilst the BBC took upon itself the responsibility of deciding what kind of tone and impression should be created and transmitted, even down to the specification of what sorts of camera shots and which objects should be given prominence. The decision to go for a 'reverential' approach, with one-third of the total footage taken up with 'symbolic' shots (focused on inanimate features of Westminster Abbey — altar cross, Coronation Plate, stonework, etc.) aimed at eliciting a sense of respectful awe and reverence, which was further communicated by the invention of an appropriate style of hushed-voice commentary by Richard Dimbleby [52]. These are all aspects of the process of communalization and of interpellation of subjects through which discourses have ideological effects. All three aspects of the process require analysis: creation and transmission of ideology and, finally, the response to it. To the extent that the viewers and listeners are won over by the discourse, with all its attractive pageantry, nostalgia and familiar symbols, they recognize themselves as the subjects addressed, and willingly consent to their 'subjection' to the sovereign power that it represents — that of the transcendent community.

It is difficult to measure the importance of civil religion and civic ritual in cementing together a concrete social formation such as a modern nation-state. There are many other important discourses which articulate together to produce the imagined community of the nation. The sense of difference — Us and Them — is fostered by international sporting events, such as the soccer World Cup and the Olympic Games, and by all those discourses in the mass media which use such terms of national difference. Their ideological effects vary over time and to the extent that the discourses are accentuated in a certain direction. For example, there seems to be some relationship between economic and political pressure, as in the economic slump of the 1980s, and the prevalence of discourses about international competition. The legitimacy of governments now depends to some degree on how far they can convince their subjects that they are holding their own or even improving their competitive position in the international league tables. However, this increases the vulnerability of the legitimation of the state and the authority of its government, because it drags them down into the sphere of the pragmatic, away from any ideologically transcendent community source. Consequently, a prime minister who cannot boast that the nation's productivity and living standards have outstripped those of comparable nations, is quite likely to direct attention to 'victories' elsewhere, at the international conference table, in battle, or sport. And, as we have seen, there is always the possibility of celebrating and remembering past glories and making them part of the imagined community at the present time.

NATION, STATE AND LEGITIMACY

In recent years there has been much talk about a 'crisis of legitimation' in capitalist states, as illustrated, for example, in the work of Jürgen Habermas and his book with that title, *Legitimation Crisis* (1975) [53]. The periodic economic crises of capitalism exacerbate the internal conflicts of interests between classes and class sections, and this creates doubts about the state's claim to power. The special position of the state derives from its role as a corporate actor, making decisions on behalf of, and speaking in the name of the whole society. This claim to legitimacy is vulnerable on two counts: firstly, if it seems to be acting on behalf of one class or section and not on behalf of the whole society; secondly, if its claim to guarantee the viability of the society is called into question by internal chaos or deterioration (e.g. riots or decaying inner cities) or by relative decline compared with other societies. Habermas's account of legitimation crises points out the inherent contradictions that face the modern capitalist state in trying to satisfy the various demands that are made on it — on the one hand there are the demands of a free enterprise, international economy, which creates strains and inequalities, but resists political intervention and restraint; on the other hand there are democratic and egalitarian demands of the people for social welfare and security programmes to protect them from economic uncertainties and structural inequalities. On the whole, Habermas tends to suggest that internationalization, both of the capitalist economic system and of the media of communication, makes it less possible for the state to appeal to national values and patriotism as a way of heading off legitimation crises. This may be true in the long term but, depending on the length and severity of periods of crisis, it may be possible for an enhanced nationalist consciousness to withstand the threats to the state's legitimacy. The forging of symbolic links between remaining traces of folk culture (memories of the heroic past, such as the Battle of Britain, or America's pioneering frontier days) can still be effective, as can other ideological devices such as those associated with civil religion. The enhanced prominence and popularity of the Royal Family, which has been fostered by the mass media in Britain during the mid-1980s economic crisis, cannot be ignored in the way that Habermas's analysis would seem to recommend. Habermas gives little weight to the importance of the continuing appeal of nationalist symbolism and the nation as an ideological community, but is more concerned with advancing understanding about the role of rational, 'undistorted' communication in the political process. His focus is on the state and not the nation.

Although Habermas has been greatly influenced in his thinking by the ideas of Max Weber, his neglect of the continuing appeal of nationalism might have been avoided if he had paid closer attention to Weber's distinction between nation and state. Weber regarded the nation as essentially a political concept which could only be defined in relation to the state, though it was not identical with it. A nation was a 'community of sentiment' that could find its adequate expression only in a state of its own, and which would normally strive to create one. It was also a subjective phenomenon — that is, it existed where people believed themselves to be one. The existence of a nation meant that a specific feeling of solidarity could be expected from certain groups of people in the face of others. The sense of solidarity was not totally subjective, because it was usually rooted in objective factors such as common language, religion, customs or political experience — its *Kultur* (culture). The nation belonged to the category of groups that Weber and other German sociologists such as Tönnies called *Gemeinschaften,* that is, which were based on a feeling of the members that they belonged together, a sentiment of solidarity. Whereas the state was an example of *Gesellschaft,* an association developed consciously for specific purposes. Whilst the nation was concerned with the realm of culture, the state's concern was the realm of power. The state could only survive in so far as it harnessed the solidary feelings of the national community in support of its power. Reciprocally, the nation could only preserve its distinctive identity, its culture, through the protection it received from the power of the state [54].

It follows from this distinction that Weber makes between nation and state, that the legitimation of the nation-state is drawn from two analytically distinct sources. If we take the state and its agencies (the *Gesellschaft* part of the nation-state), then Weber provides an analysis of its legitimacy as resting predominantly on rational-legal grounds (less on tradition and personal charisma). This sort of analysis has been developed by G. Poggi, who has traced the emergence of a shift in the rational-legal legitimacy of the state as it became more interventionist in organizing capitalist society, so that it rests more and more on 'social eudaemonic' grounds — seeking legitimacy through acts of rule that assist the economic system in producing an ever-increasing flow of goods and services for the consumer-citizen (this does not change under conservative governments, only the strategy for producing these results is different) [55].

Clearly, if this were the only source of legitimacy it would be a very precarious basis, especially in a capitalist system which suffers periodic slumps. However, as we have seen, the more the state can associate itself with the nation and identify with national sentiments, the more it can draw on the surplus of legitimacy that the nation calls forth in periods of crisis. One reason why state crises do not issue in revolutionary changes very often is that they become defined as national crises and more often than not give rise to symbolic revitalization campaigns, with appeals to traditional symbols of the nation and distancing from 'alien' elements within or outside the imaginary community.

It is interesting to note that theorists at different ends of the political spectrum have begun to give greater attention to this phenomenon. On the Left, Régis Debray draws on two sets of evidence about revolutions and crises in capitalist countries to make the claim that ethnic or national bases of stratification and legitimation are more fundamental than those deriving from mode of economic production and classes:

> First, socialist revolutionary victories have always been linked in one way or another to movements of national liberation, whether anti-colonial or not. Secondly, during every crisis in a capitalist country it has been shown that identification with the nation is stronger than class identity, even among the main mass of the people, the working class. [56]

For Debray the key question is how the nation acquires its 'sacred' character (echoing Durkheim). His answer is in terms of a philosophical anthropology that resembles some thinkers on the Right, in that he suggests that it arises out of two processes fundamental to human nature: the need to delimit our own society in time (to assign origins to it), and to delimit it in space (a fixed territory to which we belong): 'There can be no cultural identity for social individuals without distinction from and opposition to a neighbouring environment, without the drawing of lines'. The deepest layers of cultural distinction, according to this view, relate to 'peoples' not classes:

. . . horizontal class divisions appeared far later in social history than the segmentary cultural divisions of ethnos, nations and peoples. And there is an anthropological law which states that the deepest layers of a national formation or of an individual personality last longest. In both psychic and social organization, ontogenetically and phylogenetically the hard core is always archaic. This oldest stratum is always the most active — this is a fundamental and historical datum. [57]

This view is echoed in recent articles in the right-wing theoretical journal *The Salisbury Review,* such as those of Clive Ashworth, 'Sociology and the Nation', David J. Levy, 'The Real and the Royal', and Roger Scruton, 'Thinkers of the Left: E. P. Thompson' [58]. Leaving aside the politically prescriptive preference of these writers for patriotic ties over those of attachment to other ideological communities, and their various assertions about how these ties are somehow more fundamental than others, it has to be admitted that they make a useful point that sociology has given too little attention to the roots of nationalism and its enduring appeal. However, they are less helpful in offering suggestions as to how nationalisms are socially constructed and how they are mobilized as ideologies. The sense of being a people is no doubt rooted in elements of shared characteristics and common history, but these are frequently matters of dispute and contestation, linked to power struggles. Territory, language, religion, race, etc., are all sources of dispute and have to be ideologically constructed or interpreted in order to produce a sense of belonging to a national community, as a glance at the history of the peoples living in the British Isles instantly makes clear. How else can we understand the situation in Northern Ireland, or the preference of some people for Welsh or Scottish nationalism over British nationalism? The imagined community of the nation is the site of ideological contestation and power struggle. How it is imagined, the way in which its character and scope are defined, has tremendous implications for social order and social control.

The focus in this chapter has been on the processes through which discourses articulate together to create imagined communities and to produce the ideological effect of forming a social cement. In the next chapter there is a slight change of emphasis when we examine the contested and negotiated processes of social control within certain institutions.

REFERENCES

[1] A. Gramsci, *Selections from the Prison Notebooks,* London, Lawrence & Wishart, 1971, p. 328.

[2] F. Engels, 'Introduction to Socialism: Utopian and Scientific', in K. Marx and F. Engels, *On Religion*, Moscow, Foreign Languages Publishing House, 1955, p. 309.

[3] Cf. Claude Lévi-Strauss, *Structural Anthropology*, vol. 2, New York, Basic Books, 1976; Talcott Parsons, *The Structure of Social Action*, New York, Free Press, 1968 (paperback edn), and 'Durkheim's Contribution to the Theory of Integration of Social Systems', in Kurt Wolff (ed.), *Essays on Sociology and Philosophy by Durkheim et al.*, New York, Harper Torchbooks, 1964.

[4] Kai Erikson, *Wayward Puritans*, New York, Wiley, 1966.

[5] Mary Douglas, *Purity and Danger*, London, Routledge & Kegan Paul, 1966, and *Natural Symbols*, London, Barrie & Rockcliff, 1970; Roland Barthes, *Elements of Semiology*, London, Cape, 1967, and *Mythologies*, London, Cape, 1972.

[6] Louis Althusser, 'Ideology and Ideological State Apparatuses', in *Lenin and Philosophy and Other Essays*, London, New Left Books, 1971.

[7] Stuart Hall, 'Signification, Representation, Ideology: Althusser and the Post-Structuralist Debates', *Critical Studies in Mass Communication*, **2**, 2, June 1985, 91–114, pp. 104–105.

[8] J. Gordon Melton, *Encyclopaedia of American Religion*, Gaithesburg, Maryland, Consortium Books, 1979.

[9] Leo Pfeffer, 'The Legitimation of Marginal Religions in the United States', in Irving I. Zaretsky and Mark P. Leone (eds.), *Religious Movements in Contemporary America*, Princeton, New Jersey, Princeton University Press, 1974, 9–26, p. 15. the following discussion draws on Pfeffer's account.

[10] Ibid., p. 18.

[11] Ibid.

[12] Albert Bergesen and Mark Warr, 'A Crisis in the Moral Order: The Effects of Watergate upon Confidence in Social Institutions', in Robert Wuthnow (ed.), *The Religious Dimension: New Directions in Quantitative Research*, New York, Academic Press, 1979, 277–295, p. 280. Cf. Talcott Parsons, 'Social Strains in America', in Daniel Bell (ed.), *The Radical Right*, New York, Anchor Books, 1962, pp. 209–229.

[13] Will Herberg, *Protestant–Catholic–Jew*, Garden City, Doubleday, 1956, p. 87.

[14] Howard Schuman, 'The Religious Factor in Detroit', *American Sociological Review*, **36**, 1971, pp. 30–38.

[15] James A. Riccio, 'Religious Affiliation and Socio-Economic Achievement', in Wuthnow, op. cit., 199–228, p. 226.

[16] Andrew M. Greeley, 'Ethnic Variations in Religious Commitment', in Wuthnow, 1979, op. cit., 113–134.

[17] Ibid.

[18] Herberg, op. cit., p. 259.

[19] Kenneth Thompson, *Emile Durkheim*, London, Tavistock and Ellis Horwood, New York Methuen, 1982, p. 87.

[20] William Lloyd Warner, *Family of God: A Symbolic Study of Christian Life in America*, New Haven, Yale University Press, 1961, and *American Life: Dream and Reality*, Chicago, University of Chicago Press, 1953.

[21] Warner, 1961, op. cit., p. 259.

[22] Robert N. Bellah, 'Response', In Donald Cutler (ed.), *The Religious Situation, 1968*, Boston, Beacon Press, 1968, p. 389. See also his 'Civil Religion in America', *Daedalus*, **96** (Winter), 1967, pp. 1–21; and 'American Civil Religion in the 1970s', in Russell E. Richey and Donald G. Jones (eds.), *American Civil Religion*, New York, Harper & Row, 1974; and *The Broken Covenant: An American Civil Religion in Time of Trial*, New York, Seabury Press, 1975.

[23] Herberg, op. cit.; Martin Marty, 'Two Kinds of Civil Religion', in Richey and Jones, op. cit.; and Herbert Richardson, 'Civil Religion in Theological Perspective', in Richey and Jones, op. cit.

[24] V. N. Volosinov, *Marxism and the Philosophy of Language*, New York, Seminar Press, 1973 (originally published in Russian, 1930).

[25] Erikson, 1966, op. cit.; Albert Bergesen, 'A Durkheimian Theory of Political Witch-hunts with the Chinese Cultural Revolution of 1966–1969 as an Example', in *Journal for the Scientific Study of Religion*, **17** (March) 1978, pp. 19–29; see also his 'Political Witch-hunts: The sacred and the subversive in cross-national perspective', in *American Sociological Review*, **42** (April), 1977, pp. 220–233; and Bergesen and Warr, 1979, op. cit.

[26] Erikson, op. cit., pp. 138–139.

[27] Bergesen and Warr, op. cit., p. 289.

[28] Cf. J. Larrain, 'On the Character of Ideology: Marx and the present debate in Britain', in *Theory, Culture and Society*, **1**, 1, 1982, pp. 5–22, and B. Lacroix, '*The Elementary Forms of the Religious Life* as a Reflection on Power (*Objet Pouvoir*)', in *Critique of Anthropology*, **4**, 13–14, 1979, pp. 87–103.

[29] Cf. K. Thompson, *Emile Durkheim*, op. cit.

[30] Jorge Larrain, *The Concept of Ideology*, London, Hutchinson, 1979, and Paul Q. Hirst, *Durkheim, Bernard and Epistemology*, London, Routledge & Kegan Paul, 1975.

[31] Lacroix, op. cit., p. 93.

[32] Benedict Anderson, *Imagined Communities: Reflections on the Origin and Spread of Nationalism*, London, Verso, 1983, p. 131.

[33] Lacroix, op. cit., p. 95.

[34] Cf. Jurgen Habermas, *Legitimation Crisis*, Boston, Beacon, 1975; and 'Toward a Theory of Communicative Competence' in H. P. Dreitzel (ed.), *Recent Sociology*, No. 2, London, Collier-Macmillan, pp. 114–148.

[35] Althusser, 'Ideology and Ideological State Apparatuses', 1971, op. cit., pp. 127–128.

[36] Benedict Anderson, *Imagined Communities*, 1983, op. cit., p. 19.

[37] Ibid., p. 15.

[38] Ernest Gellner, *Thought and Change*, London, Weidenfeld & Nicolson, 1964, p. 169, quoted in Anderson, op. cit., p. 15, Anderson's emphasis.

[39] Stuart Andrews, *Methodism and Society*, London, Longman, 1970, p. 75.

[40] Cf. William Stafford, 'Religion and the Doctrine of Nationalism in England at the Time of the French Revolution and Napoleonic Wars', in S. Mews (ed.), *Religion and National Identity*, Oxford, Blackwell, 1982, 381–95, p. 382.

[41] William Coleridge, *On the Constitution of the Church and State*, ed. by John Colmer, London, 1976, quoted in Stafford, op. cit., p. 393.

[42] William Coleridge, *Essays on His Times*, ed. by D. V. Erdman, 3 vols., London, 1978, vol. 2, pp. 232–233, and *Table Talk*, ed. by Bohn, London, 1884, p. 274, quoted in Stafford, op. cit., p. 393.

[43] Stafford, op. cit., p. 391.

[44] Edmund Burke, *Reflections on the Revolution in France*, Harmondsworth, Penguin, 1968, p. 117, and in James Donald and Stuart Hall (eds.), *Politics and Ideology*, Milton Keynes, Open University Press, 1985, 4–6, p. 4.

[45] Ibid., p. 6. The commentary on this passage draws on Stuart Hall's, 'Study Guide' to *Politics and Ideology*, Open University Press, 1986, pp. 28–29.

[46] Louis Althusser, *For Marx*, London, New Left Books, 1977, pp. 233–234.

[47] Keith Robbins, 'Religion and Identity in Modern British History', in S. Mews (ed.), *Religion and National Identity*, op. cit., 465–487, pp. 465–466.

[48] Edward Shils, *Centre and Periphery: Essays in Macrosociology*, Chicago, Chicago University Press, 1975, p. 139.

[49] Norman Birnbaum, 'Monarchs and Sociologists: a reply to Professor Shils and Mr Young', in *Sociological Review*, **3**, 1, 1955, pp. 5–23.

[50] J. G. Blumler, J. R. Brown, A. J. Ewbank and T. J. Nossiter, 'Attitudes to the Monarchy: their Structure and Development during a Ceremonial Occasion', *Political Studies,* **19**, 2, 1971, pp. 149–171; and Robert Bocock, *Ritual in Industrial Society,* London, George Allen & Unwin, 1974.

[51] Cf., on the invention of traditions with respect to broadcasting and civic rituals, David Cannadine, 'Context, Performance and Meaning', in E. Hobsbawm and T. Ranger (eds.), *The Invention of Tradition,* Cambridge, Cambridge University Press, 1983, pp. 101–164.

[52] David Chaney, 'A Symbolic Mirror of Ourselves: Civic ritual in mass society', in *Media, Culture and Society,* **5**, 2, 1983, and in R. Bocock and K. Thompson (eds.), *Religion and Ideology,* Manchester, Manchester University Press, 1985, pp. 258–66.

[53] J. Habermas, *Legitimation Crisis,* Boston, Beacon, 1975.

[54] This summary of Weber's political sociology draws on David Beetham, *Max Weber and the Theory of Modern Politics,* London, Allen & Unwin, 1974, and Kenneth Thompson, 'Bureaucracy and the State', Study section 16 of the Open University course, *An Introduction to Sociology,* Milton Keynes, Open University Press, 1981.

[55] G. Poggi, *The Development of the Modern State,* London, Hutchinson, 1978.

[56] Régis Debray, 'Marxism and the National Question', *New Left Review,* No. 105, 1977, 25–41, p. 34.

[57] Ibid., pp. 28 and 34.

[58] Clive Ashworth, 'Sociology and the Nation', *The Salisbury Review,* Winter 1983, pp. 8–11; David J. Levy, 'The Real and the Royal', Spring 1983, pp. 17–20; Roger Scruton, 'Thinkers on the Left: E. P. Thompson', Autumn 1982, pp. 12–14.

3

Social Control

The broadest and most inclusive definition of ideology is one which makes it almost coterminous with culture, as in Therborn's statement that 'The operation of ideology on human life basically involves the constitution and patterning of how human beings live their lives as conscious, reflecting initiators of acts in a structured, meaningful world [1]. However, Therborn, like most theorists of ideology, wishes to narrow his focus, and so although he does not limit the content of ideology, he is more specific as to the operational effects of ideology. These are concerned with the 'organization, maintenance, and transformation of power in society [2]. Or, as Terry Eagleton puts it, 'By "ideology" I mean, roughly, the ways in which what we say and believe connects with the power structure and power-relations of the society we live in [3]. Most studies of ideology tend to have this focus, whether or not they make it explicit. Of course, most sets of beliefs and ritual practices have some implications for social power, even if it is only in the negative sense that they occupy mental space that might otherwise be taken up with matters more directly related to power relations. In this sense, a preoccupation with religious doctrines about the Divinity, or with international sporting rivalry, can be said to have some ideological effect. But it is when religious or other value commitments are mobilized or contested within institutional settings that it becomes clear that what is at issue is an ideological struggle over power and social control. The phrase 'battle for the mind', as used by William Sargant, in his book with that title, is probably too dramatic a term, and applies mainly to cases of radical alterations of belief, such as religious conversions and brain-washing, but it does indicate the dynamic nature of the process in its extreme form [4].

The mobilization of value commitments, which includes the formulation of persuasive interpretations of beliefs and their transmission, is the work of 'intellectuals', in the broad sense given to that term by Gramsci [5]. According to Gramsci, much of the culture and beliefs of the mass of ordinary people is composed of a 'spontaneous philosophy', which derives from a residue of conventional notions embedded in the language, common sense, and a complex of popular religion, superstitions, customary ways of thinking and acting that he called 'folk-lore'. The relationship between the 'higher' philosophy of the intellectuals and common sense had to be secured by 'politics', just as the relationship between the Catholicism of the intellectuals and that of the 'simple people' was secured by politics. There was a constant danger of a gap opening up between the beliefs of the intellectuals and those of the ordinary people:

> religion or a certain church maintains its own community of faithful people (within certain limits of the necessity of a general historical development) to the extent to which it keeps alive its faith in a permanent and organized way, tirelessly repeating the apologetics, battling at all times and always with similar arguments and maintaining a hierarchy of intellectuals who give the faith at least the appearance of dignity of thought. Every time that the continuity of contact between the Church and the faithful has been violently broken for political reasons, as happened during the French Revolution, the loss suffered by the Church has been incalculable ... . [6]

Gramsci's discussion is valuable because it emphasizes the dynamic nature of the relationship between popular and intellectual philosophies, and the contestation and struggle that is a constant characteristic of the ideological terrain. He was also aware of the implications for ideological struggle of the proliferation of different intellectual strata and professional groups within society: '. . . the state as such has no unitary, coherent and homogeneous conception. Because of this the intellectuals are separated into different strata, and again separated within each stratum' [7]. We shall concentrate on the politics of social control through ideological struggle in various institutions and the part played by different strata of intellectuals or leaders at various levels (from Sunday-school teachers to bishops, and from shop-floor union negotiators to senior managers). In the final chapter of the book we will return to the issue of differences and tensions between popular religion and 'official' religion.

SOCIAL CONTROL AND COMMUNITY OF VALUES

The link between discussions of religion and moral values as social cement and as a means of social control can be made by taking a fresh look at the seminal thesis of Alasdair MacIntyre's Riddell Memorial Lectures of 1964

[8]. In those lectures, MacIntyre made a series of highly perceptive comments on class-structure, religious outlook and moral community in England and, by contrast, America. The first part of MacIntyre's thesis about the impact of the Industrial Revolution and the accompanying urbanization that gathered momentum in the eighteenth century was fairly conventional. It stated that the effect was to destroy older forms of community, especially those features to which religion had given symbolic expression. There was the loss of structures which produced a sense of a given and largely unalterable natural order within whose limits people of different social ranks all had to live. The sense of relative continuity and stability of the social order, which made that order appear continuous with the natural order, disappeared. Whilst being aware of the danger of exaggerating the homogeneity of pre-industrial life, MacIntyre maintained that economic growth in Britain resulted in the splitting of society into new kinds of class division, in which the relations between classes were in crucial ways relations of conflict. There were intensified efforts to exercise social control in the course of these conflicts, and attempts were made to appeal to common norms and to revive the older social and moral values. But these tended to be undermined by the fact that the changing structure of society made it only too obvious that the alleged authoritative norms were in fact man-made, and that they were not the norms of the whole community to which people of all ranks were equally subject. In so far as the norms which did govern the economic, political and social relations between classes were given a religious significance, it was often the case that the justification could be seen to be special pleading for the interests of one class to prevail over those of another. The important point here is that, although there might still exist the remnants of a 'shared vocabulary of motives' which carried traces of traditional ultimate values, the real social relations between classes created mutual suspicion about the sincerity of those who appealed to such motives. Furthermore, religious practice itself became stratified along class lines to a certain extent, but not sufficiently to create separate class-based moral communities that were opposed to such an extent that they resorted to moral denunciation of each other and prevented class cooperation.

One possible objection to the first part of MacIntyre's thesis, that concerning the division of the community into rival and conflicting classes, was to ask why in that case each class did not build up its own form of moral community with its appropriate cosmic and universal justification for its attitudes as against those of other classes. The answer was that to some extent they did do this. There was the upper- and middle-class ethos, derived from the so-called 'public' schools, involving notions of service to the state and to the empire, with an emphasis on observing at least the formalities of Christian worship. There was the purely middle-class society of the mid-nineteenth century, often associated with the Nonconformist churches and with living and working according to what Max Weber called the Protestant ethic; diligence, saving and respectability were its hallmarks. It has been suggested that the skilled and supervisory section of the working-class, the so-called 'aristocracy of labour', also assimilated these values. Thirdly, there were the attempts of the working-class movement to provide its own moral and religious expressions of a universal kind, such as the Labour churches and Marxism. But, according to MacIntyre's judgement, none of these communities succeeded in integrating all classes into a shared moral universe with an accepted ultimate justification. The reason for this is to be found in the history of class relationships in England. In the earlier period of building up a labour force, the owning classes could invoke the laws of the market as divinely grounded and therefore could accept that the relations between classes should be those of relatively naked force. This was backed up by an effort to exercise social control to build more churches in urban areas, with the mission of 'civilizing' the working classes, and through promoting the socializing efforts of Sunday schools. However, with the emergence of a skilled and organized labour force and in a period of relative economic prosperity there began to develop, from 1865 onwards, a more marked tendency towards relations of class cooperation. This had implications for the moral sphere in English society, which have continued to this day. As MacIntyre puts it:

It appears there is a moral change corresponding to these economic and social changes, not only in the relations between middle-class employers and workers but also in the relations between the middle classes and the landed classes. It is centered upon the quite new emphasis from the middle of the nineteenth century onwards in English life upon what I intend to call 'the secondary virtues'. If you read any book produced from the late nineteenth century onwards about English life written by an Englishman from an English point of view, the virtues which are said to be characteristic of the English are a pragmatic approach to problems, co-operativeness, fair-play, tolerance, a gift for compromise, and fairness. I call these secondary virtues for this reason, that their existence in a moral scheme of things as virtues is secondary to, if you like parasitic upon, the notion of another primary set of virtues which are directly related to the goals which men pursue as the ends of their life. The secondary virtues do not assist us in identifying which ends we should pursue. The assumption made when they are commended is that men are already pursuing certain ends, and that they have to be told to modify their pursuit of these ends in certain ways. The secondary virtues concern the way in which we should go about our projects; their cultivation will not assist us in discovering upon which projects we ought to be engaged. [9]

To summarize the second and more original part of MacIntyre's thesis, therefore, it is that class conflict in Britain developed to a sufficient extent to provoke suspicion about any appeal to ultimate values and general theories to justify such values, but it did not produce a total moral split between classes, because there remained some agreement about certain 'secondary virtues', or procedural norms, that made class cooperation possible.

This general thesis about the development of religion and moral values and their connection with class relations, and therefore with power and social control, will be explored further. However, it is worth noting that MacIntyre also sought to clarify his thesis by considering another objection to it. It could be objected that if it was true, as he claimed, that urbanization and industrialization produce secularization, why did this not happen in the United States? Although America does not have an Established church, unlike England where even in the 1980s more than half the population still claim some sort of affiliation to the Church of England, actual church attendance and active membership is much higher than in England. At the beginning of this decade only 13 per cent of the adult population of England were registered church members, whereas in the United States roughly 70 per cent claimed membership of a church or synagogue and 40 per cent of the population attended church at least once a week [10]. One possible explanation lies in the history of successive waves of immigration into America and the way in which ethnicity and religious affiliation have combined to provide a sense of community and identity for generations of Americans. This was the explanation offered by Lenski, whose study of religion in Detroit found that the influence of religion on social, political and economic attitudes was relatively independent of membership of social class [11]. Similarly, Herberg's study *Protestant–Catholic–Jew*, maintained that the churches were the historical vehicles for instilling American values, incorporating ethnic communities into a broader national community of values. The core native American values were those of individual achievement and equality, the social ideals of the American Revolution, which occurred before the process of class differentiation was accelerated by the

Industrial Revolution. The result was that the differentiation of classes occurred *within* a value-system, and it was accompanied by a high degree of geographical mobility and a sense of fluid social mobility. Individual Americans felt that they could rise in the social scale on the basis of their own abilities, and as this aspiration and belief was validated by the shared value-system of America, the United States was able to provide a communal unity which linked social strata vertically and not just horizontally. Contemporary American religion functions as an expression of those links. Thus, MacIntyre concludes that,

> . . . the difference between the secularization of English society consequent on industrialization and the lack of secularization in American society is in the end a product of two different class structures, one of which allows for there being a national community of values and the other of which only allows that national community of values to exist at the level of what I call secondary virtues. [12]

Whether MacIntyre is right to suggest that there is a difference of class structure and of rates of social mobility between classes in the two societies is debatable. However, at the ideological level his account is more persuasive. It does provide an explanation for the differences in religious practice between the two countries, and of the links between national ideology and sub-cultures associated with ethnic groups and classes. Americanism as a national ideology has more plausibility than British nationalism because it is more attuned to the need to surmount sectional divisions and makes a direct appeal to shared ultimate goals and values, whereas the British equivalent rests on secondary virtues. However, both societies' ideologies also rest on an appeal to solidarity and national identity by constituting themselves as ideological communities that are superior to competitors or in opposition to an alien Other.

It follows from what has been said that the 'Dominant Ideology Thesis' of classical Marxism, and the common culture thesis of functionalist sociology, are more plausible for America than for Britain, according to MacIntyre's thesis. The history of America has followed a trajectory that allowed for a greater degree of incorporation of different classes into a set of ultimate values that are more widely shared than in Britain. It is easier for dissatisfied groups in America to appeal to a set of shared values to express their grievances than is the case in Britain. This is illustrated by the fact that America's ultimate values are explicitly enshrined in legal formulae, such as the Constitution and Bill of Rights, and aggrieved groups or individuals seek legal redress for their grievances. In Britain the appeal is more likely to be couched in terms of negotiations about 'custom and practice', as we will see when we turn to a discussion of the ideology of shopfloor industrial negotiations. Similarly, in the case of attempts by the Church to intervene in economic and political matters in Britain, the bishops are now criticized for 'taking sides' and being dangerously controversial if they make moral judgements rather than phrasing their comments in terms of the 'secondary virtues'.

If it is true that the second half of the nineteenth century saw the emergence of the key ideas of British society as being those typified by the secondary virtues, arising out of the necessity of class compromise and class cooperation, this was not without a struggle. The struggle continued even though it became institutionalized through the organized labour movement. But it was even more pronounced in the earlier part of the nineteenth century, when the ruling class did try to impose their own virtues and values on other groups, using religion as a class weapon, and the churches and Sunday schools were key sites of ideological struggle.

CHURCHES, SUNDAY SCHOOLS, AND CONTROL IN THE INDUSTRIAL REVOLUTION

Both Althusser and Durkheim emphasized the 'social cement' aspect of ideology — the way in which discourses and practices such as those of religion reproduced social relations involving submission to a superior social force. They both stressed that ideology was embedded in material practices, such as rituals and other social practices. Thus, to take an example from English religious history, one of the means of transmission of the ideological domination of the ruling class in eighteenth-century England was through the organization and practices of the Church of England, not just through preaching and teaching. Even the lay-out of the seating in churches, where the best pews were rented to the socially superior classes, cemented the social order in a particular ideological form. However, in periods of crisis, such as that of the Industrial Revolution and the French Revolution, ideology had to be mobilized in a much more active fashion in order to maintain social control. It is not surprising, therefore, that this was also a period of frantic church reform, with new forms of religious organization being created in an attempt to transmit the 'calming' or 'civilizing' influence of religion to the working classes [13]. But there was a limit to what could be achieved through the agency of a Church whose strength as a source of ideological stability had rested on its embeddedness in a traditional social order. Despite the state's encouragement to the Church to extend its ministry in the new working-class urban areas, much of the adult population was never attracted back into church membership. The state began to place more emphasis on socializing the young through new educational institutions.

Althusser has asserted that the dominant Ideological State Apparatus in pre-capitalist societies was the Church, which included within its functions educational and cultural elements, whereas in capitalist industrial society the educational system is the overwhelmingly dominant ISA. If he had examined the British case in more detail he might well have concluded that the key transitional or bridging role in this development was performed by the Sunday schools during the first three-quarters of the nineteenth century, until the state stepped in to fill in the gaps left by the inadequate system of voluntary day schools with the Elementary Education Act of 1870. (Even then, elementary education did not become compulsory until 1880.) Whilst the state's efforts to revivify and reform the Church of England and to build more churches in urban areas met with very little success in bringing working-class adults under the Church's influence and control, the Sunday schools attracted the majority of children into membership by the middle of the nineteenth century. In the period from 1801 to 1851, the percentage of working class children attending Sunday school in England rose from 13.8 to 75.4, whereas the participation of working class adults in religious activities was limited to a small minority [14].

The low level of participation by working class adults in religious activities was a matter of constant concern to the ruling class in Britain. Nevertheless, there were times when the religious activities of some sections of the working class were perceived as a threat to social order, particularly the itinerant evangelism of the Methodists, which challenged the paternalistic Angelican establishment. Anglican bishops denounced it as a species of religious radicalism, whereas some contemporary radical leaders saw Methodism as a conservative deflection from political objectives. Historians have come to different conclusions about which tendency it most represented, depending on their own ideological leanings. The important point is that religion was at the centre of ideological contestation in this period. It was the time of the 'making of the English working class' as E. P. Thompson called it, before the later nineteenth-century class compromises had been arrived at and prior to the institutionalization of class cooperation on the basis of the 'secondary virtues'.

It is no coincidence that the same period that was judged to be vital for working class development, according to a radical historian such as Thompson, was also described as the most crucial in the modern history of English religion by an ecclesiastical historian (W. R. Ward) [15]. According to Thompson it saw the 'making of the working class' when, as a result of their common experience 'in the years between 1780 and 1832 most English working people came to feel an identity of interests as between themselves, and as against their rulers and employers' — a class consciousness [16]. However, as Thompson points out, there were certain peculiarities about that consciousness. Although it was subjected to the formative influence of the productive relations common to all wage-earners in a capitalist mode of production, the class consciousness of the English working class had its own peculiar characteristics. The way in which they interpreted their experience was affected by the cultural resources at their disposal and the social context in which they existed, with its particular institutional structures. One of the most important features of English culture and social structure was its religious formation — including traces of the bitter struggles involving religious dissent and political radicalism in the seventeenth century. It is not surprising, therefore, that the social upheaval of the Industrial Revolution and the formation of the English working class should be marked by ideological struggles that once again involved disputes about religious beliefs and practices. There was an attempt to re-integrate the working class into a dominant ideology of shared religious values, with the hope that it might be possible to win their continuing consent to being subject to a system in which they were exploited and their interests were not democratically represented. But the social changes of urbanization and industrialization undermined the traditional community basis, including the church's parochial system, and new religious movements outside that system, such as Methodism and the Evangelical movement, were viewed with suspicion by the authorities. Nevertheless, it was these new religious movements that achieved most success in attracting the working class. Historians have presented different views as to whether, or to what extent, religion did serve as an agency of social control in this period.

This issue provides a classic test case for competing theories and explanations of ideology. A common problematic adopted by many of those who examine this case, which fits in with many recent Marxist theories of ideology, but pre-dates them and can be found in the writings of nineteenth century French historians who contrasted England with revolutionary France, poses questions about why English working-class consciousness was not more revolutionary. Answers tend to be sought in terms of the existence of structures, including structures of discourses and of intellectual leadership, which impeded the development of such a consciousness. According to the French historian Élie Halévy, the answer did not lie in England's political or economic institutions, but in English religion, especially the effects of Methodism and the wider Evangelical movement on the thinking of the political leaders of a revolution. Halévy's thesis was that Methodism and Evangelicalism channelled off the potentially revolutionary leadership of the working class [17]. In so far as they maintained a political allegiance and involvement in organized labour movements their preference was for reformist policies and class compromise. Some historians have argued that these values characterized the leadership stratum of skilled workers that emerged in the second half of the century and who they refer to as the 'labour aristocracy'. There is some dispute about how far this more skilled and educated section of the working class adopted middle-class values, but it does seem to have been the case that they were inclined to enter into industrial negotiations with a commitment to the secondary virtues, which were expressed in terms of the characteristic appeal to 'custom and practice' [18].

E. P. Thompson's thesis about the social control functions of Methodism suggested it had a broader impact than Halévy's thesis proposed. According to Thompson, Methodism was ideologically effective because: (a) it served the exploiting class's interest in exercising social control through indoctrination of the workers, especially through the Sunday schools; (b) it could 'offer to the uprooted and abandoned people of the Industrial Revolution some kind of community to replace the older community-patterns which were being displaced'; (c) it offered compensation for disappointed this-worldly hopes, including political hopes, by emphasizing the after-life — it was the 'chiliasm of despair' [19].

Other historians have disagreed with Thompson's account of the ideological functions served by Methodism and Evangelicalism. Gilbert maintains that Thompson over-emphasized the repressive 'utility' of Methodism in inculcating a 'work discipline' to the exclusion of the more attractive obverse effect of its legitimation of self-improvement and economic endeavour. Thompson is accused of writing with some distaste for Methodist beliefs and values, evidently out of a conviction that the best they could offer was 'consolation' to those who felt 'defeated and hopeless'. Gilbert suggests that this was a minor function in the total ideological impact of Methodism; its most widespread appeal was to groups whose economic and social positions were improving, and it echoed the aspirations rather than the despair of the working classes. The issue of which of the ideological functions served by Methodism and Evangelicalism was the most important cannot be resolved by a simple appeal to neutral evidence because such evidence is never completely independent of any conceptual structure. This is the reason why so much consideration has to be given to *theories* of ideology. However, such evidence can clear away over-simplification and generalizations that are too broad. A comparison of the different accounts provided by historians such as Gilbert and Thompson reveals that certain functions relate to some groups of Methodists but not to others, and that this also varied over time. For example, until the demoralizing introduction of the powerloom had its impact on handloom weavers after the Napoleonic Wars, weavers joined Methodism in large numbers and found there an 'overall congruity' between the religious culture and the spirit of independence and self-reliance which characterized their socio-economic situation. Methodism appealed most to those skilled manual workers who were prominent in the first stage of Britain's Industrial Revolution, while it was unable to repeat its success with the factory workers of the Victorian period. It has been suggested that this helps to explain why the Methodist contribution to trades unionism was strongest in mining areas and weakest in areas dominated by cotton operatives [20].

Different ideological functions of Methodism and Evangelicalism have been emphasized by historians, depending on whether they gave more emphasis to the social control perspective, like Thompson, or preferred to view these religious movements as expressions of working class cultures and aspirations. For example, Gilbert stresses the positive function of the chapel communities, which were largely created and sustained by working class lay members; whereas Thompson sees them as instruments of the middle class for exercising social control and instilling discipline in the working class. The same contrast, between an imposed social control perspective and an approach which emphases the ways in which working-class religion was an expression or translation in a religious idiom of people's own aspirations and communal values, occurs in accounts of the functions served by the Sunday-school movement, and with regard to the relations between Methodism, popular beliefs and working-class culture [21].

The issue as to whether the potentially revolutionary working class were controlled by being successfully incorporated into a religious belief system that was dominated by bourgeois ideology, is not easily resolved by an appeal to historical 'facts'. We have noted that active participation in religious activities by working class adults was relatively low, and even the case for the influence of Sunday schools does not provide unequivocal evidence of incorporation. Although E. P. Thompson is successful in showing that the middle-class founders and management committees of Sunday schools often had that purpose in mind, Laqueur concludes that the Sunday-school teachers, a large proportion of whom were working class, and the parents, did not share that intention. Many Nonconformist Sunday schools seemed to have grown out of the demand from within the working class for basic education and the transmission to children of the values of the 'respectable' working class, or 'labour aristocracy' — industry, thrift, self-discipline, improvement, communalism and egalitarianism. Laqueur sees such Sunday schools as genuinely popular institutions that promoted working-class culture, and therefore akin to trades unions, friendly societies, cooperatives, building societies, savings banks, and various institutions for intellectual improvement. Certainly the authorities in the Church of England and in the Wesleyan branch of Methodism feared that the Sunday schools could have such effects, and in the 1820s they made strenuous efforts to prohibit the teaching of writing to Sunday school pupils. The original Methodist emphasis on the values of equality of all people before God and the community of believers within the Church, resonated with the remaining traces of democratic-egalitarian and communal-activist values of the working class, and were a constant source of acute tension within Wesleyanism as the representatives of bourgeois values — the clergy and leading laymen — promoted centralization, inegalitarianism, and support for the existing social order. This led to splits, and some branches of Methodism, especially the Primitive Methodists, were closely connected with radical working-class movements and supported political action [22]. Even E. P. Thompson, who paints a negative political picture of Methodism, admits that some Methodists did display confrontationist, class-conscious, proletarian values in the early nineteenth century [23].

Perhaps the best conclusion that can be drawn from the evidence about religion and social control in the Industrial Revolution is that there was no straightforward, one-way transmission of bourgeois ideology which could result in the incorporation of the working class into a common culture or dominant ideology, if by this we mean that there was a consensus about certain ultimate beliefs and values. The working-class communities were not 'clay', open to the imprint of whatever values were pressed upon them, nor were the values exclusively class related or derived. Firstly, as we have suggested with regard to Sunday schools, the learning and organizational abilities developed there could be used in working-class trades union and political organizations, even if these did tend to be more reformist than revolutionary. Secondly, the actual contents of the 'texts' used in Sunday schools — scriptures and hymns — were open to a variety of interpretations. They included highly symbolic and potent images of various sorts, and these could be adapted for use by political radicals and the hymns were sung at Chartist rallies. Finally, it is an over-simplification to suggest that the Methodist and Evangelical stress on individual conversion and individual moral responsibility corresponded to the values of bourgeois individualism in economics and politics [24]. Methodism and Evangelicalism were not uniformly opposed to collectivist social action and there were fierce disputes within their ranks over politics, resulting in a series of controversies and secessions from Wesleyan Methodism in the second quarter of the nineteenth century [25]. The opportunities offered by chapel culture for self-improvement and the development of leadership qualities resulted in Methodism and the Sunday schools producing many of the leaders in radical politics and trades unions. But, as Robert Moore found in his study of Methodism in the mining communities of north-east England, 'while Methodism did produce political leaders amongst working men it did not produce leaders who would articulate and pursue class interests as such' [26]. Methodists tended to divide their society into the saved and the unsaved, or the good and the bad, but not into middle and working classes. As Hempton puts it, 'Methodism both fostered radicalism and opposed it, and the roots of this paradox are to be found in the religious mind itself, with its acceptance of authority on the one hand, and its desire to have justice and fair play on the other [27].

There are many ways of conceptualizing the ideological effects of religion in the period of the Industrial Revolution. Some of the effects were the intended consequences of the efforts of the middle and upper classes to exercise social control over the working class. Others were the unintended consequences of the efforts of working-class people to satisfy their various needs, including needs that were religiously generated as well as those that arose from the disruption and hardship of capitalist industrialization. Among the many ideological effects of religion that have been suggested, the following summary contains the most notable: 'the opium of the people' (Marx); a compensation for those who suffer in this life through the promise of higher status in the spiritual realm (Max Weber); a transitional ideology helping the worker to adjust to the requirements of capitalist industrialization or 'modernization' by inculcating a religiously sanctioned work-discipline (Weber); creating a form of community that eased the passage from traditionally based community (*Gemeinschaft*) to a more impersonal, rational and contractually based social order (*Gesellschaft*) (Gilbert and Semmel) [28]. It has also been suggested that religion resulted in the channelling off from the working class of its potentially revolutionary leadership (Halévy), and the formation of a reformist tendency among the 'aristocracy of labour'. Whether it is possible to go further and make a convincing case that such strata were incorporated into the ideology of the dominant class (the 'dominant ideology thesis') is debatable [29]. Perhaps the most that can be established is that they were prepared to enter into compromises and negotiations on the basis of a set of shared 'secondary virtues' (MacIntyre).

The lesson that emerges from an examination of this classic case in debates about religion and ideology is that reality is usually more complex than historians or theorists of ideology suppose. As far as the historical evidence is concerned, I would agree with Hempton's conclusion that the relationship between Methodism and popular politics was a good deal more complicated and colourful than the 'sterile debates surrounding the Halévy thesis would indicate', and that proper attention must be paid to the local economic, religious and social setting [30]. With respect to theories of ideology, it has to be admitted that is is doubtful whether an adequate general theory yet exists that can generate anything more than very broad hypotheses for the purpose of explaining such complicated events. Most current theories of ideology tend to be either extremely abstract, as E. P. Thompson has complained, or where they are more concrete and specific, they tend to relate to recent trends in mature capitalism and so offer little guidance for studying events in earlier periods [31]. However, some of the ideas and concepts deriving from these theories are relevant, particularly those inspired by Gramsci's discussions of hegemony, the role of intellectuals (including 'organic intellectuals', leaders of thought in various classes and specialist spheres of activity), and of the different layers of culture that constitute a class's consciousness [32]. These ideas find their nearest parallel in the sociology of religion in the work of Max Weber [33]. Weber has been criticized for not having developed a more dynamic view of the 'elective affinities' between certain types of ideologies and various social strata. The relationship sometimes appears rather passive, unlike Gramsci's picture of the ideological terrain as the site of contestation and struggle. Gramsci's dynamic view was a great improvement over the older 'economistic' Marxist theory, according to which religion was viewed as mere superstructure, or a cultural 'transmission belt' for the interests of the dominant class. His guiding principle of 'articulation' envisaged a looser set of relationships in which there was no pure dominant ideology descending from above, nor a pure working-class ideology emanating from below, but rather complex forms of interaction of political, cultural and ideological negotiation within and between classes. This picture corresponds most accurately to the situation of religion in the Industrial Revolution, where there was constant struggle and negotiation, not only between classes, but also within classes and religious bodies. The struggles within Methodism and over control of Sunday schools illustrate this very well.

IDEOLOGY AND CLASS IN VICTORIAN ENGLAND

Although class relations became more stable and marked by a greater degree of compromise and cooperation from the middle of the nineteenth-century, it would be wrong to attribute this to the successful incorporation of the working class into a dominant bourgeois ideology. There was no single dominant ideology pressing down from above on the working class and functioning to maintain ruling-class control. The ideological terrain is best viewed as a complex of discourses, which articulate together in ways that are affected by the particular cultural resources available and the distribution of power. The overall outcome can then be described in terms of its ideological effects in various regions of social life. In the religious sphere, as we have seen, Methodism and the Sunday schools had a mixed ideological impact. Their teaching and organization were functional for developing time and work discipline that had been lacking in early factory workers. They also taught certain leadership skills and a sense of responsibility that were useful for foremen and master-craftsmen in a system of work organization where there was widespread sub-contracting of tasks to leaders of work gangs. In politics, the influence of religion on the working class had the effect of producing leaders who were reformist and prepared to enter into negotiations within institutionalized procedures. By the middle of the nineteenth century the economy was producing a more general relative prosperity, and in the political sphere radical Chartism had declined, whilst the middle class had gained some of its objectives with the Reform Bill of 1832. It has been suggested that these were the conditions that led to a mellowing of ideology and the consolidation of a set of cultural traits that constitute what we know as Victorianism: domesticity and family; respectability; improvement; and conventional Christian morality [34]. Evangelical morality penetrated even some of the aristocracy and led them to oppose the interests of the manufacturing section of the ruling class in so far as they seemed to threaten to undermine the family, hence Lord Ashley's efforts to limit the hours of work in factories. Respectability included the values of thrift, self-help and independence; it was closely linked to 'improvement', which included the eighteenth-century rationalist devotion to intellectual improvement, and Protestantism's and Evangelicalism's emphasis on progressive sanctification of the individual [35]. Conventional Christian morality buttressed the sanctity of the family, patriarchal authority and the regulation of sexuality. It also promoted self-discipline and condemned idleness and licentiousness, and led to constant efforts to stamp out the remaining elements of the old plebeian culture, such as fairs and blood sports, not to mention the temperance movement's campaigns against drunkenness. Philanthropy was a voluntary activity, and malingerers had to be distinguished from the deserving poor when charity was dispensed [36]. Behind all these various ideological tendencies, according to some sociologists, there lay the fundamental value of individualism, which Weber had discussed in terms of an affinity between Calvinism and the spirit of capitalism. Others have attempted to trace it back even further than the rise of Calvinism in the sixteenth century — Macfarlane, for example, traces the origins of English individualism as far back as the thirteenth century [37].

The question that has to be answered is whether this constituted a dominant ideology, and was this ideology shared by the dominant class and the working class? Different answers have been given to this set of questions. Abercrombie *et al.* in *The Dominant Ideology Thesis*, maintain that it was the ideology of the *ascending* class, a bourgeois ideology aimed at the destruction of traditionalism and the creation of opinion favourable to capitalist industrialism. They believe it was successful in becoming the ideology of the dominant class, and that the older values of the landed class became marginalized. This conclusion is opposed to that of Perry Anderson, who argued that the English bourgeoisie failed to perform one of the historical roles assigned to it by Marxist theory, which was to formulate an ideology that destroys traditionalism [38]. Because the aristocracy transformed itself into a capitalist class with interests aligned to those of the bourgeoisie, the latter did not need to develop a coherent ideology as part of a process of trying to overthrow the older ruling class. The latter maintained its place within the broader dominant class of industrialized capitalism and protected its landed and financial interests. Consequently, there was no new dominant bourgeois ideology, and bourgeois utilitarianism was merely a 'sectional rationale of the workings of the economy' and mid-century liberalism was a weak political version of this [39]. Anderson tends to differentiate aristocratic cultural hegemony from ideology, which he conceives more narrowly as a hegemonic political philosophy. Although this narrow definition of ideology is not one that we follow in this book, his notion of cultural hegemony is compatible with our perspective, which sees the ideological terrain as a complex of discourses articulating together to produce a particular form of cultural dominance. According to Anderson's account, the working class was not penetrated by this dominant aristocratic culture, unlike the middle class, but it did set limits to the scope of its challenge to the existing order. For example, aristocratic paternalism seemed more sympathetic towards the suffering of the industrial workers than did the harsh values of bourgeois factory owners, and it did issue in legislation offering some protection against the worst excesses of exploitation.

Abercrombie *et al.* do not deny that the there was a synthesis of bourgeois and aristocratic cultures, and that the bourgeoisie became gentrified, aping the lifestyle and social mannerisms of the old landed aristocracy. However, they emphasize the triumph of bourgeois ideology, which they regard as a single, coherent and unified set of beliefs, whereas Anderson chronicled the post-1850 defeat of the 'entrepreneurial ideal' by the counter-revolution of the ideals of empire, aristocracy, gentry and rural romanticism. This latter theme is one that has received more support recently in the work of Martin J. Weiner, *English Culture and the Decline of the Industrial Spirit, 1850–1980*, which traces the present weakness of the British economy to the long-term decline of central aspects of the very ideology that Abercrombie *et al.* insist became dominant [40].

The problem of resolving the question as to whether there was a dominant ideology is partly due to the tendency to look for a single dominant ideology, linked to a particular class, when what is needed is a careful mapping of the complex of discourses that articulate together to produce ideological effects. There needs to be an appreciation of the fluid and contested nature of the ideological terrain, so that we are alerted to the possibility that the power balance that produces one set of ideological effects at a particular moment, may be tilted in another direction within a relatively short period of time. This approach is all the more necessary when what is being discussed are such very broad and general values as 'individualism', 'respectability', or the existence of an 'entrepreneurial' ideal. It is quite possible that the articulation of various bourgeois and aristocratic values tilted, within a few decades of the mid-nineteenth century, from a short-lived position in which an entrepreneurial spirit favourable to manufacturing interests began to gain the ascendancy, to a position in which ideals of empire, aristocracy, liberal professions, gentry and rural romanticism came to the fore — ideals that were unfavourable to the long-term interests of British manufacturers.

There has recently been a call for more research to establish to what extent a specifically industrial version of the entrepreneurial ideal was ever formulated or advanced towards a hegemonic position, and, if so, to determine when it was defeated [41]. An important factor may have been the influence of the public schools and the removal of impediments to members of Non-conformist churches entering civil and military service, and Oxford and Cambridge universities. Unlike the Dissenting Academies, which had been the main educational institutions for members of Non-conformist churches, the public schools and the ancient universities promoted values that were antithetical to manufacturing industry. Consequently, as Leys suggests,

> The most significant result of the repeal of the Test and Corporation Acts, and the subsequent abolition of patronage in the civil service, may not have been just to lift an obstacle to the assimilation of the new capitalist class into the old landed class, as has been widely noted; it may have also removed one of the few structural forces which had hitherto channelled middle-class talent into industrial occupations and the education necessary for their pursuit [42].

However, the influence of educational institutions and cultural leaders such as the intellectuals could not have been decisive for changing the balance of ideological forces unless economic structural conditions had been conducive. British industry dominated world markets because it was the first industrial state, and so manufacturing interests did not have to strive for ideological dominance in order to create favourable conditions for the accumulation of capital. Other European states had to develop scientifically and technically oriented mass educational systems and cultures for the purpose of breaking into world markets dominated by Britain. In Britain educational and professional values were more like those of the gentry and of a traditional society, with a conservative attitude that working-class children should not be educated to rise above their class origins, in contrast to Germany, where technical and scientific education was almost universal. Joseph Kay reported in 1850 that in Germany he 'constantly found the children of the highest and of the lowest ranks sitting at the same desk' [43]. This relatively democratic and technological educational ethos was very different from that in Britain. Educational discourses and practices in Britain were more concerned with social control, hierarchy and deference. James Donald, drawing on the ideas of Foucault and Donzelot about 'bio-politics' and the 'policing of families', has shown that even in their most progressive forms, such as the ideas for state intervention to promote national efficiency of the Fabian leaders Sidney and Beatrice Webb, at the end of the nineteenth century, they were still concerned with 'policing' the population, through surveillance and the gathering of information [44]. Bright working-class children were to be segregated from the majority of children and given special education, whilst the remainder, who were regarded as dangerous or in danger, needed other forms of care and control. These policies were not just the result of educational ideologies, in the narrow sense of sets of ideas or philosophies organized in certain linguistic codes, and circulating historically within particular discursive fields, such as government reports and debates, journalism and tracts on pedagogy. They were also the result of the development of what Foucault calls 'human sciences' in the practices of schooling — theories of child development and changing pedagogic techniques. As Donald put it:

The distinction is not between discourse and practice, but between the discourses embodied in ideological representations and those embodied in these sciences and techniques. These latter are integral to the routines of schooling in ways that cannot altogether be explained in terms of ideology. They are comparable to other regimes of knowledge studied by Foucault. In *Madness and Civilization* (1965), for example, he showed how the principles evident in the organization of asylums were formalized in the discipline of psychology; in *Discipline and Punish* (1977), he examined how the new science of penology determined the design of prisons, the activities of the agents working in them, and the ways in which their inmates were categorized and treated. These forms of knowledge were not so much representations of the institutional practices as their very motor [45].

Foucault answers the question posed by Althusser, as to how individuals take up positions within a social world that already exists, by explaining that this subjectification is achieved through the subtle mechanisms of power within institutions and apparatuses of knowledge. However, this emphasis on schooling as a form of social regulation is not incompatible with an interest in the symbolic processes by which schooling produces certain forms of subjectivity, as Donald demonstrates. Educational reformers in nineteenth-century Britain were increasingly concerned with 'policing' the population through surveillance and welfare, and with ensuring that the content of education produced the right types of people. The latter concern became prominent towards the end of the nineteenth century, when 'national efficiency' became the watchword, as there were fears about the 'fitness' of the population to compete internationally and to undertake the responsibility of an 'imperial race' [46]. Hence, social regulatory mechanisms were instituted in practices such as setting criteria for classifying children, and by keeping detailed records of the child's development and home life. The curriculum too embodied a particular ordering of the symbolic sphere, which established hierarchical relations between different forms of knowledge, and in turn this generated a network of subject positions in relation to those hierarchies — it defined what it was to be educated, cultivated, discriminating, clever, literate, and so forth. It made it possible for this system of differentiation and social hierarchy to be presented as a natural consequence of the personality and intellectual aptitudes of the people who occupy those subject positions.

It is interesting to note that research on selection interviews for candidates to one of the older professions in Britain (Army officer) found that great emphasis was laid on uncovering 'natural leadership' character traits, and that these seemed to coincide with speech and attitude patterns of candidates who had received a public school education [47]. This fits in with Perry Anderson's claim that the hegemony of aristocratic culture and values was maintained even after the ascent of the new middle class to share political power in the nineteenth century by the creation of an educational institution — the public schools — which socialized the sons of the rich into the culture and behaviour of the 'gentleman'. Anderson attributes great importance to the period of military–industrial imperialism from 1880 to

1914. This 'apotheosis of British capitalism', he argues, strongly influenced the cultural emphasis on 'leadership', and a concept of leadership which maximizes the difference between rulers and ruled, stressing the basis of leadership not in skill but in style, and values not of training or theory but natural, essential, aristocratic superiority. Another way of putting it would be to say that the public schools set out to build character and instil leadership qualities through moral training, emphasizing the 'secondary virtues' characteristic of conventional Anglican religion, and shorn of the excesses of Evangelical enthusiasm. Correspondingly, the subordinate classes are instilled with attitudes of deference and a sense that there is a natural hierarchy based on innate characteristics. Needless to say, this ideological hegemony has been contested, and its viability has been undermined by increasing signs of lack of success, from the failures of the officer class in the First World War, to the growing awareness of the decline of the British economy. In recent years there has been an attempt by politicians to revive Victorian values, which seems to include an effort to restore a spirit of technological and industrial enterprise. However, as we have seen, it is doubtful that such an ascendancy of these values ever existed in Britain. Even in the present crisis, the prospering sectors of the economy appear to be those concerned with finance and property rather than manufacturing industry, and it is in the former sectors that the old elite are still the governing establishment [48]. As for working-class education, the watchword of 'national efficiency' has become prominent again, as it was in the period of intensifying international competition at the end of the nineteenth century. It remains to be seen whether, this time, it will lead to greater democratization, or simply result in more 'policing' of the population into predetermined social positions.

CONTROL AND WORK

There are clear parallels between Foucault's ideas about social regulation through institutional disciplines, as applied to schools, and Max Weber's ideas about bureaucracy in work organizations and the state [49]. Weber was concerned with the problem of how social cohesion or discipline could be maintained in a capitalist state in the absence of supernaturalist presuppositions. He suggested that the disciplines of the monastery provided the model for discipline in the factory. These disciplinary practices were the basis for the spirit of capitalism, which he summed up as 'exact calculation'. Rational administration involved the measurement of human performance, as exemplified by double-entry book-keeping, capital accounting, legal codification and examination systems. Such administration was epitomized by bureaucratic organization, in which tasks were broken down into specialized components, the performance of those tasks was governed by detailed rules and subjected to surveillance by occupants of offices in a hierarchy, the scope of whose authority and competence was clearly specified [50]. Like Weber's model of bureaucracy, with its hierarchy of offices, chains of command and specialization of functions, Foucault's view of social control in capitalist society emphasized surveillance, classification and measurement of the population through various institutions.

It would seem that disciplinary practices within institutions are more important than shared values for maintaining social order in capitalist society, according to Weber and Foucault. This is the conclusion drawn by Turner and other critics of Marxist theories of a 'dominant ideology' and sociological theories that stress the importance of shared values for the maintenance of social order and for eliciting citizens' and workers' consent to their dominance by the state or by capitalist employers. However, we have suggested that both symbolic processes *and* regulatory practices were important in producing ideological effects in education. The same case can be made for work organization. Littler has argued that we lack a vocabulary of concepts for discussing ideological relationships in industrial organization [51]. In particular, he agrees with Burawoy's suggestion that we need to distinguish between 'legitimacy' and 'consent' [52]. There are various levels of legitimacy, ranging from general cultural norms which create overarching patterns of legitimacy orientation, such as the right of the employer to own and market the product (i.e. property rights), to organization-based legitimacies exemplified by ideologies of technocracy and management expertise. Managers spend time and effort in sustaining these ideologies, and they enter into the constant negotiations over control within each enterprise. However, the achievement of compliance depends upon specific trade-offs and interactions which have little to do with large-scale legitimations. There is bargained consent, as is shown by the occasions when a foreman's instruction is resisted, even though the overall framework of legitimation may not have been questioned.

Another way of pursuing this theme is by reference to Gerth and Mill's concept of a 'vocabulary of motives' [53]. This notion suggests that in any cultural setting there are certain acceptable motives for action (what others have called 'legitimizing principles') which are, in turn, embedded in the characteristic discourse (sometimes referred to as the world-view or ideology) of that culture. Negotiations over rules, including the making of new rules, their interpretation and adaptation, must engage with common vocabularies of motives or legitimizing principles. This has been described by Anselm Strauss as a 'negotiated order' — the outcome of a process in which the participants deploy such power and legitimizing resources as they

possess in their attempts to change or interpret the rules in their favour [54].
However, there is an inherent asymmetry in this process within capitalist
enterprises. As Armstrong *et al.* put it:

> Whereas managerial ideology comprises a relatively coherent
> body of thought, comprehensively expressive of management
> interests, this is far from the case with the fragmentary counter-
> ideology available to workers. Whereas managers can justify their
> actions, at least to themselves and often to workers as well, by
> citing the principles of managerial prerogative and profitability,
> either of which will justify virtually any rule change, workers must
> ordinarily make use of legitimizing principles which are relatively
> specific. [55]

It is worth noting that this contrast between the more intellectually
formulated and coherent ideology of the dominant class in the workplace,
and the fragmented and more concrete 'philosophy' of the subordinate
class, is reminiscent of the distinction drawn by Gramsci, which was quoted
at the beginning of this chapter. It also corresponds to the findings of
research on workers' images of society. Westergaard and Resler argue that
these tend to be fragmentary, inchoate and incomplete rather than coherent and internally consistent [56]. A fully developed and consistent class
consciousness, involving a systematic rejection of the ideology of the
dominant class, is rarely in evidence; more often there are fragmentary
elements of class consciousness, usually most prominent in times of severe
disputes and crisis, uneasily co-existing with acquiescence to a 'negotiated'
version of the ideology of the dominant class [57]. Workers are usually to be
found appealing to 'custom and practice' as a legitimation for their
resistance to management's rule changes or rule interpretations, rather
than appealing to alternative, society-wide ideologies. Often in their appeal
to 'custom and practice' the workers seek to ground the legitimacy of their
case in the principle that it is reasonable to expect people, including
managers, to behave consistently. They may also appeal to some of the
secondary elements in managerial ideology, such as the claim that
managers act not solely in their own interest but on behalf of the whole
community or as arbitrators of competing interests. It is increasingly the
case that managers, whether in publicly or privately owned organizations,
phrase their goals in terms of such ideologically appealing notions as the
professional ideal of 'service', or 'efficiency' in delivering corporate growth
or community benefits, rather than in terms of 'profit'. 'However', as
Armstrong *et al.* point out, 'these apparently diverse aims all depend upon

increasing the economic return from the employment of labour and in that sense are equivalent to the profit motive as far as the effect on the work-force is concerned'. Similarly, the use of notions such as 'productivity' and 'enlarging the cake' for the benefit of all concerned, serve to avoid contentious distributive arguments associated with the term 'profit' [58].

Without going so far as to re-introduce the notion of a single dominant ideology, it is still possible to accept that the language, codes and discourses of the wider culture are ideologically weighted in favour of managerial interests. The positive overtones of the term 'efficiency' make any resistance to measures that are aimed at increasing profitability seem like an advocacy of 'inefficiency'. Terms such as 'demarcation dispute' and 'restrictive practice' are conveniently loaded with pejorative implications that undermine the workers' case for resistance to control. Armstrong *et al.* also catalogue some even more unobtrusive legitimizing principles, such as the appeal to 'self-evident common sense' — 'of course' the supervisor should be paid more than those being supervised, and 'of course' the workers should do other work when the machines breakdown. This taken-for-granted, common-sense knowledge needs to be investigated by an ethno-methodological approach that renders these organizational practices as 'anthropologically strange' [59].

Another approach that can be effective in decoding the discourses that have such ideological effects is that of historical and cross-cultural comparison. Each society, or social formation, has its own peculiar cultural patterns and trajectory of structural development, even though it may be classified as having the same mode of production as others. British capitalism has ideological peculiarities or particularities that differentiate it from other capitalist societies, just as it also has had a different path of development. Many sociological generalizations have been faulty because they have failed to appreciate these differences. This is especially the case with regard to Marxist theories of the 'labour process', which seek to explain management strategies for control of labour and the design of work tasks. The British experience has been taken as the typical model of industrialization, whereas, as Kumar has shown, 'Seen from the perspective of the present, a century and a half later, the British case stands out as unique in almost every important respect' [60]. It was unique in its gradualness, in its bourgeois nature, in its unplanned nature and the lack of state control, and in its freedom from foreign influences. In Britain there was a substantial commercial class that promoted industrialization, whereas in France, Germany and Italy there was a forced industrialization imposed on society by the state. Similarly, the pattern of worker resistance to management control varied to a degree not recognized by some Marxist writers on the labour process such as Braverman. For example, as Littler points out, in the USA the waves of immigration created a labour process increasingly organized on the basis of ethnically and linguistically segregated work groups, and this splintering affected the potential for worker resistance to labour rationalization [61]. Consequently, the process of bureaucratization and scientific management ('Taylorism') advanced much more quickly in America at the end of the nineteenth century, whilst in Britain older patterns such as sub-contracting of labour persisted up to the First World War.

In the British Industrial Revolution there was little need for a new dominant ideology for the purpose of controlling the labour process and legitimating managerial authority. Whilst there is much truth in historians' descriptions of the recalcitrance to factory life of British workers and of the need to foster new work disciplines (as E. P. Thompson maintained that Methodism did), much of this was concerned with time-discipline and absenteeism (the custom of 'Saint-Monday' — treating Monday as a saint's day holiday — for instance). Capitalists maintained traditional forms of subordination and dependency within a system of sub-contracting of labour, using master craftsmen to recruit and control apprentices (e.g. iron-masters and shipwrights), family heads to recruit members of their family as assistants (e.g. spinners), and gang bosses to hire and control their own gangs (e.g. dock-workers, and the butty system in coal mines). This had implications for the development of ideology in the early British trades unions and among the so-called 'aristocracy of labour', as many of the unions were primarily associations of internal contractors and they often used the union to develop a set of rules regulating the work done by helpers and underhands [62]. Such groups may have been penetrated by middle-class ideology or values of respectability and morality relating to lifestyle, which was the suggestion about the aristocracy of labour, but there was no new dominant ideology within the work sphere. The development of such an ideology really only became an issue as a result of the Great Depression of 1873–96, which lowered profit margins and forced employers to consider the question of labour efficiency. In the first half of the nineteenth century, productivity was seen solely in terms of long hours and the speed of machines. Even when the problem of labour utilization became an issue there was still strong resistance in Britain to adopting American ideas such as Taylorism. Some influential Quaker employers, such as Edward Cadbury, who was the leading management intellectual, opposed Taylorite methods because they entailed excessive speeding up, debased the workers, and could cause serious conflict between capital and labour. Littler also points to other reasons, such as the limited mass market for engineering goods until the armaments drive of the First World war, and the fact that British employers 'rejected a high-wage strategy which was an essential element of the American model bacause of class-based notions of appropriate wage-levels' [63].

What energes from such cross-cultural comparisons is that strategies of control and their ideological legitimiations differed in significant respects between societies with the same capitalist mode of production, and with respect to the period in which changes occurred. Britain persisted longer with traditional patterns of control and ideology than some other societies. This is also illustrated by the prestige and persistence of the ideology of the liberal professions within British work organizations. Child *et al.* note the effect of this on the status and power of engineers in Britain compared with their conterparts in Germany, in an aptly titled paper, 'A Price to Pay? Professionalism and Work Organization in Britain and West Germany':

> British engineers (and their counterparts in other functions) are often qualified and specialized in terms of the perceived needs of occupational (professional) groups, or those of academic disciplines; rather than in terms of the needs of the tasks to be done in particular industrial sectors, as is to a large extent the case with engineers in Germany [64].

Furthermore, the system of values or ideology of professionalism in Britain, in so far as they relate to the service orientation derived from the traditional liberal professions of law and medicine, whilst serving the wider social-status interests of the professionals, may have little practical relevance to the work to be done, and so deny engineers a central role in the organization. As Child *et al.* put it with respect to engineers in British manufacturing industry: 'Indeed, in so far as a "service" stance is carried over from the long-established and prestigious professions of law and medicine, specialists in industry will feel it appropriate to "assist" production while maintaining a distance from any active involvement in it' [65].

Once again we see that the uniquely long-drawn-out industrialization of Britain, and its particular class and cultural system, have affected the ideological complex. Intellectual groups, such as the liberal professions, developed particular discourses and values ('philosophies' as Gramsci would say), which continue to colour the vocabularies of motives that are drawn on to mobilize support for, or resistance to, social control. It is interesting to note that the growth of the professions in Britain coincided with the process in France that Foucault described in terms of 'bio-politics'. In the French case it referred to a switch in the state's conern with its citizens, in the seventeenth and eighteenth centuries, away from a consideration of subjects only in terms of their rights and duties *vis-à-vis* the state, and towards a new concern with the growth and care of the population, and the monitoring and welfare of individuals. This direct state involvement in 'bio-politics' did not develop in Britain until the nineteenth century, as we have discussed with regard to state education. Before that, in Britain, the traditional professions were allowed to develop a certain amount of autonomy and freedom from external control as a result of political conditions in which the state was beginning to take more responsibility for its citizens' welfare and protection against maltreatment, but delegated the control of this function to professional associations. Furthermore, because the members of the professions were drawn from the higher classes or gentry, they could demand autonomy and freedom from close supervision in their work; this was justified in terms of an ideology of service, the eschewing of the cash nexus characteristic of capitalism, and the claim that practitioner–client relations rested on trust. This professional ideal, and its associated social status and prestige, have remained strong in Britain. Ideologies of professionalism still persist in many white-collar and service occupations, and workers in those occupations use them to demand autonomy and to resist close control. The success of such appeals varies between occupations. The fastest-growing professions, such as engineers and other technical professions, exhibit a split between an elite, who exercise some of the functions of the capitalist, and the majority who have much less freedom from control. Many of these technical professionals find themselves under threat of being de-skilled by the fragmentation of their tasks and the substitution of machinery. They are likely to turn to trades union organization rather than old-style professional associations to defend their interests, and ideologically they are more like other wage-earners. However, for those who continue to perform some management functions, or who are relatively sheltered from threats to their professional status and autonomy, traditional ideological elements still have a strong appeal.

Despite the spread of bureaucratic rationalities and discipline, as discussed by Weber and Foucault, the symbolic processes and discourses that constitute British work ideologies contain substantial traditional elements that enter into negotiations over workers' consent to the rules and the authority of those who control them. They also continue to function as legitimating principles for resisting control, which may explain why British work organization is frequently criticized for its 'inefficiency' of for being out of date.

CONTROL AND THE DOMINANT IDEOLOGY THESIS

Critics of the 'dominant ideology thesis' direct most of their criticisms against the notion that social order within a capitalist system has to be maintained by incorporating the working class into the ideology of the dominant class, or into a common set of values. We have suggested that it is not necessary to think in terms of *the* ideology of a class, but that it is more accurate to speak of complexes of discourses and practices which have ideological effects. However, provided this is kept in mind, we need not be excessively rigorous and there need be no objection to following the conventional practice of referring to sets of beliefs which have implications for people's perception of their position in society and of the nature of society, as ideologies. However, among the critics of the dominant ideology thesis there are some, such as Abercrombie, Hill and Turner, who argue that for feudalism and early capitalism there was a fairly coherent dominant ideology which, partly because of the appratus of transmission, incorporated the dominant classes but not the subordinate classes [66]. They maintain that religion and the family (which built up and retained capital) were two of the main agencies of transmission of a relatively coherent ideology in the dominant class(es). Whereas in late capitalism, religion has declined even among the dominant classes, and the modern capitalist economy no longer depends on the existence of a class which retains capital within the family structure. As for the working class, although the agencies of transmission of ideology have become more effective, such as the mass media and education, the ideology of the dominant class contains many disparate elements and inconsistencies. The state is expected to assist in promoting capital accumulation, but state intervention tends to dilute the rights of property-owners to exploit their ownership without interference or regulation. Furthermore, the state is also expected to protect and promote the welfare rights of its citizens, which may require compromise of some material interests of sections of the dominant class. The political discourses of liberal-democracy and the welfare state contain an ideology of state neutrality as between different classes and sectional interests. The ideological effect of these discourses is to mask the central role of the state in the accumulation and reproduction of capital in a way which systematically promotes the interests of those who own or control capital [67].

Another region or sphere of ideology where there are disparate elements is that of managerial ideology, as we have already noted with respect to the two elements derived from the tradition of the liberal professions — a service orientation and a claim to professional expertise. It is generally believed that the former element has declined relative to that of the claim to technical expertise [68]. However, there is some evidence that British management ideology has maintained a particular version of the superior qualities of those in authority, which is not as much concerned with technical expertise as is the case in other capitalist societies, such as America. In a study by Theo Nichols of the ideology of directors and senior managers in Britain he found little evidence of a change from a traditional managerial ideology based on notions of 'leadership qualities' and the general diffuse superiority of the leader/manager towards a more bureaucratic ideology of a 'technocratic' type based on an appeal to technical expertise [69]. When asked what made a good manager, most respondents thought that 'character', 'personality', social skills and personality characteristics in general were more important than technical skills. By far the largest category of response contained reference to 'leadership' or some supposed aspect of this, such as 'commanding respect'. These social skills and personality traits correspond to those inculcated and valued in the elite educational institution of the public schools, which Perry Anderson picked out as the key agency by which the rising middle class were socialized into the values of the aristocracy and gentry. It is still the case that the management heirarchy in many sectors of the economy is itself stratified in terms of public school education: the higher the level in the hierarchy, the larger the proportion of those with a public school education. The business elite, like the elite in many other sectors of British society, has had this particular formative educational experience and been inculcated into its values [70].

The conclusion to be drawn is that there is evidence of the dominant class in Britain, or some of its elite sections, being socialized into a set of shared values, some of which were drawn from the culture of the aristocracy and gentry. However, these exist alongside disparate elements deriving from other sources, such as the technocratic and bureaucratic rationality characteristic of large-scale organization in all modern societies, and the peculiarly British attachment to a set of 'secondary virtues' of pragmatism, fair-play, tolerance and compromise. The working class is dominated more by the regulatory disciplines of institutions than it is by having its commitments mobilized by ideological processes. Nevertheless, its perceptions of the social order and the possibilities for imagining a different order and aspiring to bring it about, are affected by cultural factors, including the residue of older cultural elements that form what Gramsci called the 'spontaneous philosophy' of the common people. The securing of the relationship between the 'higher' philosophy or culture of the intellectuals and the 'spontaneous philosophy' and culture of the common people is a political process — 'cultural politics'. Our discussion of Methodism, Sunday schools, and the control of work, have dealt with aspects of this in certain institutional processes, particularly with respect to the ideologies of leaders or 'intellectuals' in those institutions. In the next chapter we will undertake a closer examination of 'popular' cultures, including popular religion, and their relationship to higher or intellectual philosophies and professionally produced cultural creations.

REFERENCES

[1] Goran Therborn, *The Ideology of Power and the Power of Ideology*, London, Verso, 1980, p. 15.

[2] Ibid., p. 1.

[3] Terry Eagleton, *Literary Theory*, Oxford, Blackwell, 1983, p. 14.

[4] William Sargant, *Battle for the Mind*, London, Pan Books, 1959.

[5] A. Gramsci, *The Modern Prince and Other Writings*, trans. by Louis Marks, New York, International Publishers, 1957. (I have used this early English edition, which includes selections from the 'Prison Notebooks', except where the English translation published by Lawrence & Wishart, 1971, seemed significantly superior.)

[6] Ibid., p. 72.

[7] Ibid., p. 75.

[8] A. MacIntyre, *Secularization and Moral Change*, London, Oxford University Press, 1967.

[9] Ibid., p. 24.

[10] Cf. *U.K. Christian Handbook*, London, Evangelical Alliance/Bible Society/Marc Europe, 1983.

[11] G. Lenski, *The Religious Factor: A Sociological Study of Religion's Impact on Politics, Economics and Family Life*, Garden City, New York, Doubleday Anchor Books, 1963.

[12] MacIntyre, op. cit., p. 34.

[13] Cf. Kenneth A. Thompson, *Bureaucracy and Church Reform: The Organizational Response of the Church of England to Social Change, 1800–1965*, Oxford, The Clarendon Press, 1970.

[14] T. W. Laqueur, *Religion and Respectability: Sunday Schools and Working Class Culture, 1780–1850*, New Haven, Yale University Press, 1976, p. 44, and in R. Bocock and K. Thompson (eds.), *Religion and Ideology*, Manchester, Manchester University Press, 1985, p. 135. Cf. also, A. D. Gilbert, *Religion and Society in Industrial England: Church, Chapel and Social Change, 1740–1814*, London, Longman, 1976, pp. 59–68.

[15] E. P. Thompson, *The Making of the English Working Class*, Harmondsworth, Penguin, 1968, and W. R. Ward, 'The Religion of the People and the Problem of Control, 1790–1830', *Studies in Church History*, **8**, 1972, pp. 237–257.

[16] E. P. Thompson, op. cit., p. 12.

[17] Élie Halévy, *A History of the English People in the Nineteenth Century*, 3 vols., Harmondsworth, Penguin, 1938.

[18] Cf., for a discussion of some of the issues and evidence regarding the labour aristocracy, Robert Q. Gray, *The Labour Aristocracy in*

Victorian Edinburgh, Oxford, The Clarendon Press, 1976, and his *The Aristocracy of Labour in Nineteenth Century Britain, c. 1850–1900*, London, Macmillan, 1981; G. Crossick, 'The Labour Aristocracy and its Values', *Victorian Studies*, **19**, 3, 1976, pp. 301–328; H. F. Moorhouse, 'The Marxist Theory of the Labour Aristocracy', *Social History*, **3**, 1, 1978, pp. 61–82.

[19] E. P. Thompson, op. cit., pp. 416–419.

[20] David Hempton, *Methodism and Politics in British Society, 1750–1850*, London, Hutchinson, 1984.

[21] Cf. Laqueur, 1976, op. cit., and K. Thompson, 'Religion, Class and Control' in R. Bocock and K. Thompson, (eds.), op. cit., pp. 126–153.

[22] E. J. Hobsbawm, *Labouring Men: Studies in the History of Labour*, London, Weidenfeld & Nicolson, 1957.

[23] E. P. Thompson, 1968, op. cit., p. 430.

[24] For an instructive discussion of different sorts of individualism, individuality and individuation, in relation to social change and ideology, see N. Abercrombie, S. Hill and B. S. Turner, *The Sovereign Individuals of Capitalism* (forthcoming). (I am grateful to the authors for allowing me to read this work in manuscript.)

[25] Cf. Hempton, op. cit.

[26] Robert Moore, *Pitmen, Preachers and Politics*, Cambridge, Cambridge University Press, 1974.

[27] Hempton, op. cit., p. 216.

[28] Cf. Bernard Semmel, *The Methodist Revolution*, London Heinemann, 1974; and Max Weber, *The Protestant Ethic and the Spirit of Capitalism*, London, Allen & Unwin, 1930.

[29] For a critical review of the evidence for this thesis see N. Abercrombie, S. Hill and B. S. Turner, *The Dominant Ideology Thesis*, London, Allen & Unwin, 1980.

[30] Hempton, op. cit., p. 216.

[31] E. P. Thompson, *The Poverty of Theory*, London, Merlin, 1978.

[32] A. Gramsci, *Selections from the Prison Notebooks*, London, Lawrence & Wishart, 1971.

[33] Max Weber, *The Sociology of Religion*, trans. by E. Fischoff, London, Methuen, 1965.

[34] Abercrombie *et al.*, *The Dominant Ideology Thesis*, p. 102.

[35] Ibid., pp. 103–104; G. Best, *Mid-Victorian Britain 1851–75*, London, Weidenfeld & Nicolson, 1971; and T. R. Tholfsen, *Working-Class Radicalism in Mid-Victorian England*, London, Croom Helm, 1976.

[36] Abercrombie *et al.*, 1980, op. cit., p. 104; G. Stedman-Jones, *Outcast London*, Oxford, Clarendon Press, 1971.

[37] A. Macfarlane, *The Origins of English Individualism*, Oxford, Blackwell, 1978.

[38] Perry Anderson, 'Origins of the Present Crisis', *New Left Review*, **23**, 1964, pp. 26–53.

[39] Ibid.; p. 41; and Abercrombie *et al.*, 1980, op. cit., p. 95.

[40] Martin J. Weiner, *English Culture and the Decline of the Industrial Spirit, 1850–1980*, Cambridge, Cambridge University Press, 1981.

[41] Colin Leys, 'Thatcherism and British Manufacturing', *New Left Review*, **131**, May/June 1985, pp. 5–25.

[42] Ibid., p. 22.

[43] David Landes, *The Unbound Prometheus*, Cambridge, Cambridge University Press, 1969, p. 342; quoted in Leys, op. cit., p. 21.

[44] James Donald, 'Beacons of the Future: Schooling, Subjection and Subjectification', in V. Beechey and J. Donald (eds.), *Subjectivity and Social Relations*, Manchester, Manchester University Press, 1985, pp. 214–249. Cf. also, J. Donzelot, *The Policing of Families*, London, Hutchinson, 1979; and works by Michel Foucault: *Madness and Civilization*, New York, Random House, 1965; *The Birth of the Clinic*, London, Tavistock, 1973; *Discipline and Punish*, London, Allen Lane, 1977; *The History of Sexuality*, vol. 1, London, Allen Lane, 1979; *Power and Knowledge*, edited by C. Gordon, Brighton, Harvester, 1980; *The Archaeology of Knowledge*, London, Tavistock, 1972.

[45] Donald, op. cit., p. 217.

[46] Ibid., p. 223.

[47] Cf. Graeme Salaman and Kenneth Thompson, 'Class Culure and the Persistence of an Elite: The Case of Army Officer Selection', *Sociological Review*, **26**, 2, May 1978, pp. 283–304.

[48] Cf. P. Stanworth and A. Giddens (eds.), *Elites and Power in British Society*, Cambridge Cambridge University Press, 1974.

[49] I am indebted to Bryan Turner for making clear the extent of these parallels. Cf. Bryan S. Turner, 'Nietzche, Weber and the Devaluation of Politics: the problem of state legitimacy', *Sociological Review*, **30**, 3, 1982, pp. 367–391.

[50] Cf. Max Weber, *The Protestant Ethic and the Spirit of Capitalism*, London, Allen & Unwin, 1930; and repeated references to these themes in his three-volumed work *Economy and Society: an Outline of Interpretive Sociology*, New York, Bedminster Press, 1968.

[51] Craig R. Littler, *The Development of the Labour Process in Capitalist Societies*, London, Heinemann Educational Books (now Gower), 1982, p. 39.

[52] Michael Buraway, *Manufacturing Consent*, Chicago, University of Chicago Press, 1979.
[53] H. H. Gerth and C. Wright Mills, *Character and Social Structure*, London, Routledge & Kegan Paul, 1954.
[54] Anselm Strauss *et al.*, 'The Hospital and its Negotiated Order', in F. G. Castles *et al.* (eds.), *Decisions, Organizations and Society*, Harmondsworth, Penguin, 1971, pp. 103–123.
[55] P. J. Armstrong *et al.*, 'ideology and Shop-floor Industrial Relations: Theoretical Considerations', in Kenneth Thompson (ed.), *Work, Employment and Unemployment*, Milton Keynes, Open University Press, pp. 121-139.
[56] J. Westergaard and H. Resler, *Class in Capitalist Society: A Study of Contemporary Britain*, London, Heinemann, 1976.
[57] Cf., for a discussion of this 'negotiated' version, Frank Parkin, *Class, Inequality and Political Order*, London, MacGibbon & Kee, 1971.
[58] Armstrong *et al.*, op. cit., p. 127.
[59] Ibid., p. 136.
[60] K. Kumar, *Prophecy and Progress: The Sociology of Industrial and Post-Industrial Society*, Harmondsworth, Penguin, 1978, p. 126.
[61] Littler, op. cit., p. 4; and H. Braverman, *Labour and Monopoly Capital*, New York, Monthly Review Press, 1974.
[62] Littler, op. cit., p. 68.
[63] Ibid., p. 65.
[64] John Child *et al.*, 'A Price to Pay? Professionalism and Work Organization in Britain and Germany', in *Sociology*, 17, 1, 1983, pp. 63–78.
[65] Ibid., p. 66.
[66] Abercrombie *et al.*, 1980, op. cit., p. 158.
[67] C. Offe, 'The Theory of the Capitalist State and the Problem of Policy Formation', in L. N. Lindberg, *et al.* (eds.), *Stress and Contradiction in Modern Capitalism*, Lexington, Mass., 1975, pp. 125–144.
[68] Abercrombie *et al.*, 1980, op. cit., p. 136; and John Child, *British Management Thought*, London, 1969.
[69] Theo Nichols, *Ownership, Control and Ideology*. Cf. also the discussion in Kenneth Thompson, 'Organizations as Constructors of Social Reality (1)', in G. Salaman and K. Thompson (eds.), *Control and Ideology in Organizations*, Milton Keynes, Open University Press, pp. 216–236, especially 224–231.
[70] Cf. P. Stanworth and A. Giddens (eds.), *Elites and Power in British Society*, op. cit.

4

The Archaeology of Culture

Although the debates about the dominant ideology thesis have stimulated a greater interest in historical analysis among sociologists, the search for *the* dominant ideology in a particular period has been less fruitful. At the end of the debate it often appears that there was a shifting balance of ideological forces from period to period, between fractions of the politically dominant class, and between different institutions or ideological regions. It is relatively easy to discern dominant ideologies within institutions, such as managerial ideologies, but it is not so easy to see how more general and disparate elements of culture relate together to form an ideological ensemble. Much of the debate over Anderson's claim that the culture of the aristocracy triumphed over that of the bourgeoisie tends to revolve around disputes about which cultural elements were most widespread and important, whether they were the aristocratic traditional values, inhibiting philosophical speculation and promoting respect for hierarchy and deference to authority, the bourgeois value of 'individualism' in its various manifestations, or the 'secondary virtues' listed by MacIntyre. As the authors of *The Dominant Ideology Thesis* admit, because these cultural elements are very diffuse and general, the claim that they constitute an ideology is very difficult to verify [1].

Once we leave the confines of specific institutions, in which disciplinary practices and their ideological legitimations are relatively clear-cut, the diffuse field of culture is more difficult to analyse in terms of its ideological constitution. This is particularly the case with respect to the culture of everyday life or 'popular culture'. There are many layers of different cultural elements within such cultures: residues of old philosophies and practices, folklore, superstitions, popular religion (as distinct from intellectually formulated, orthodox religion), and so on. In modern society, this popular culture is also penetrated by appropriated elements of mass media culture, which have become lodged in the common consciousness — hence the popularity of 'golden-oldies' programmes, particularly at times of nostalgic remembrance, such as Christmas and New Year's Eve. Gramsci's discussions of the relationships between intellectual philosophies and 'spontaneous' philosophies of the common people, and between official Catholicism and popular religion (including folklore), are helpful in indicating ways of theorizing the connections between, on the one hand, cultural layers and processes and, on the other, social and political strata (classes, class fractions, leadership elites, intellectuals) and their relationships.

Gramsci's use of the concepts of hegemony and consensus is instructive because it refers not to a static condition but to an active and continuing process, to the always contested ideological regulation of relations between classes. The ruling bloc in a society does not depend solely on the coercive domination of the state over the subordinate classes, but offers intellectual leadership, which entails taking account of, and making concessions to, the ideas and interests of the subordinate classes. The intellectuals, whether the traditional intellectuals (the liberal professions, including the clergy, writers and academics), or the subaltern, organic, intellectuals of the rising strata in various institutions (managers, technicians, functionaries), must connect with the common-sense or popular culture of the subordinate classes. These sedimented layers of common-sense or popular culture constitute the 'sub-stratum of ideology'. Gramsci illustrates the problem of the cementing function of ideology by reference to religion, as we have already noted:

This problem is that of preserving the ideological unity of the entire social bloc which that ideology serves to cement and unify. The strength of religions, and of the Catholic Church in particular, has lain, and still lies, in the fact that they feel very strongly the need for the doctrinal unity of the whole mass of the faithful and strive to ensure that the higher intellectual stratum does not get separated from the lower. The Roman church has always been the most vigorous in the struggle to prevent the 'official' formation of two religions, one for the 'intellectuals' and the other for the 'simple souls'. [2]

The ideological ensemble is likely to be drawn from various cultural sources, therefore, not simply from that of the dominant class or class fraction; it will include cultural elements drawn from other classes and class fractions. The contents of such a complex ensemble can never be specified in advance, and it will depend on a whole series of historical and national factors, and also the relations of forces existing at a particular moment in the struggle for hegemony [3]. In so far as there is ideological unity in such a diverse cultural complex it is secured by its articulating principle, which is provided by the class or stratum that is exercising leadership/hegemony. Ideological struggle is concerned with efforts to put such an articulating principle into effect, which may entail 'disarticulation' and 'rearticulation' of the various cultural layers or discursive chains. Gramsci gives some clues as to what will determine the victory of one hegemonic principle over another, when he declares that a hegemonic principle does not prevail by virtue of its intrinsic logic but rather when it manages to become a 'popular religion' [3]. He explains what this means by stating that a class which wishes to become hegemonic has to 'nationalize itself', and that:

> the particular form in which the hegemonic ethico-political element presents itself in the life of the state and the country is 'patriotism' and 'nationalism', which is 'popular religion', that is to say it is the link by means of which the unity of leaders and led is effected. [4]

In other words, although the various elements of an ideological complex are derived from different sources and classes, their hegemonic ideological effect results from that articulating principle which manages to resonate with the widest range of elements of popular culture. Some of our earlier discussions of civil religion and nationalism provided examples of attempts to create a 'collective national-popular will' (what we called an 'ideological community') by articulating various discourses and elements of popular culture. Bearing these discussions in mind, and Gramsci's example of the relation between official Catholicism and popular religion, we will now look in more detail at some elements of popular culture and their ideological articulation.

HEGEMONY, POPULAR CULTURE AND THE WORKING CLASS

It is perhaps significant that the area of study in which Gramsci's ideas have been most enthusiastically taken up is that of popular culture studies, particularly the history of popular culture in the nineteenth century. One reason is that Gramsci provides a framework of analysis which cuts across the division in the study of popular culture between 'culturalists', who are primarily interested in the analysis of 'lived' cultures and experience, drawing inspiration from such seminal works as E. P. Thompson's *The Making of the English Working Class* and Raymond Williams's *Culture and Society 1780–1950*, and 'structuralists', primarily interested in the analysis of texts using methods inspired by Saussure's linguistics, Lévi-Strauss's structural anthropology, and Althusser's Marxism [5]. More importantly, Gramsci's Marxism reveals the political significance of popular culture, whilst avoiding the error of 'economistic' Marxism which suggested that the relationship between economy, class and culture was a mechanical and one-way process. The two-way nature of the process, according to Gramsci, meant that the subordinate classes did not passively acquiesce to the efforts of the dominant class to exercise cultural leadership and win consent to their authority. Consistent with his 'willed' conception of consciousness, Gramsci believed that in assenting to dominant conceptions and norms the subordinate classes also worked on (or 'negotiated') them. We will discuss some of the implications of this aspect of Gramsci's perspective, before considering applications of his other important concept, that of 'common sense' or 'spontaneous philosophy' of the people.

The importance of viewing popular culture as a 'negotiated order' can be illustrated by the example of accounts of changes in popular culture during the nineteenth century. The most thorough-going application of this Gramscian perspective, although it does not focus much on the entertainment elements of popular culture, is Robert Gray's essay, 'Bourgeois Hegemony in Victorian Britain' [6]. Gray rejects Perry Anderson's thesis that the industrial bourgeoisie failed to establish its hegemony and impose its values, and that it was the values of the landed aristocracy that triumphed. According to Gray, the industrial bourgeoisie *ruled through* the aristocracy, and he believes this is demonstrated by the fact that the effect of the ideological complex was to secure the progress of bourgeois industrialism. We have already questioned whether this was the long-term effect, and Weiner's study, *English Culture and the Decline of the Industrial Spirit* provides evidence that the ascendancy of industrial values was short-lived, if it ever occurred. Furthermore, Gray himself admits that hegemony cannot be located in groups of leading intellectuals — the professionals or 'urban gentry', as he calls them, who were permeated by 'genteel' values and status concerns. These urban gentry were 'very much to the force' in propagating a common ideology that sought to counter the moral dangers of urban industrial society but it had a distinctively traditional character:

The second distinctive feature is a paternalistic colouring, the attempt to reproduce in urban society the harmonious social hierarchy supposed, in a highly ideological view of social conflict, to characterize a lost rural world. Both features reflect their social location as bourgeois intellectuals, distanced from the realities of industrial production. [7]

Gray also stresses that the attempt to impose ideological hegemony had to proceed through cultural negotiation, particularly after the emergence of an aristocracy of labour stratum in the second half of the century. This process resulted in the adaptation of such values as thrift and respectability, to take account of the aspirations and experience of the working class, particularly the organized and articulate sections — the labour aristocracy. The articulation of these adapted values was largely the work of 'subaltern intellectuals', leaders of thought and opinion among middle strata, ranging from white-collar and skilled workers to elementary schoolteachers and lay-preachers. Leaders of organized labour were another important grouping of 'intellectuals' in the broad Gramascian sense, and their significance increased later in the century, especially with the advent in the 1870s of working-class representation in local and parliamentary government. 'Their mode of life and, therefore, ideology were quite different from those of the bourgeoisie, and hegemony over them, and over the subordinate classes generally, depended on the representation within the hegemonic ideology of "a number of elements which transcribe the way classes other than the hegemonic class live their conditions of existence" ' [8].

The advantage of the Gramscian stress on negotiation is that it avoids some of the deficiencies of theories of culture which put a one-sided emphasis on either the 'social control' or the 'social expression' functions of culture. Social control theories tend to regard all cultural processes in terms of the manipulative efforts of the dominant class to exercise moral leadership and dominance over the subordinate classes. Often they are couched in terms of the explanation of a non-event — failure of the working class to develop a revolutionary consciousness. The contents of Victorian music-hall songs have been interpreted in terms of their contribution to this function [9]. By contrast, social expression theories explain culture in terms of its function as a social expression of the experience and way of life of a class. Hence, for example, music hall has been viewed as the culture of the urban 'folk', and as giving voice to the consciousness of the class that patronized it [10]. Bernard Waites has cogently criticized this notion on the grounds that:

Notions of class expression in themselves entail major difficulties when (as they often do) they presume a homology (or structural resemblance) between a social class and an individual social actor. To treat classes as if they were persons on the historical stage, each with a specific psyche or consciousness, flies in the face of all the evidence we have that no class in history has ever resembled a social actor. Of course, late nineteenth-century working-class people did share attitudes and values and these were mediated through certain music-hall songs, but this is far from saying that music hall expressed a class consciousness. In the multitude of norms held and practised within the working class there was no entity resembling an inner state to be expressed. [11]

Gramsci's perspective allows us to view popular culture as a terrain of negotiation and exchange between classes and groups. Furthermore, popular culture as a whole, has some of the characteristics that Gramsci described as constituting the 'spontaneous philosophy' and common-sense of the people: a heterogeneity of elements, not rationally and systematically ordered as more 'intellectual' philosophies and institutional normative structures tend to exhibit. Popular culture, like common-sense, contains many traces of past struggles and of elements that were once more prominent; these do not necessarily disappear when new cultural forms come into vogue. Although it was once fashionable to draw a sharp contrast between the popular pursuits of eighteenth-century, largely rural society, and a new pattern of working-class leisure in urban, mid-Victorian Britain, Hugh Cunningham and others have emphasized the continuities between the earlier plebeian culture and that provided by commercial entertainment in the later period [12]. The ruling classes in urban areas certainly endeavoured to bring the old plebeian culture under control, and to introduce more rational and improving recreational activities. They also attempted to organize the leisure of the working class in such a way as to re-build a sense of community that they hoped would counteract class divisions. But, as Cunningham concludes, many of these efforts were not very successful; old aspects of culture lived on in new or adapted forms (as in circuses, music-halls, race-meetings and fairs), or the commercial effects were such as to make entertainments even more class-specific. Culture did not simply express the experience of classes, as though emanations of their present conditions of existence (economic and political relations), it also helped to construct and constitute social collectivities such as classes. The working class was made and re-made by the superimposition of layers of culture and the re-articulation of their discursive elements. As Gareth Stedman Jones puts it:

> If the 'making of the English working class' took place in the 1790–1830 period, something akin to a remaking of the working class took place in the years between 1870 and 1900. For much of the cluster of 'traditional' working-class attitudes analysed by contemporary sociologists and literary critics dates, not from the first third, but from the last third of the nineteenth century. This remaking process did not obliterate the legacy of the first formative phase of working-class history, so well described by Edward Thompson. But it did transform its meaning. In the realm of working-class ideology, a second formative layer of historical experience was superimposed upon the first, thereby colouring the first in the light of its own changed horizons of possibility. The struggles of the first half of the century were not forgotten, but they were recalled selectively and re-interpreted. The solidarity and organizational strength achieved in social struggles were channelled into trade union activity and eventually into a political party based upon that activity and its goals. The distinctiveness of a working-class way of life was enormously accentuated. Its separateness and impermeability were now reflected in a dense and inward-looking culture, whose effect was both to emphasize and to articulate its position within an apparently permanent social hierarchy. [13]

The English working-class, and the English class system, were constituted (within the bounds set by economic relations) on the basis of the layers of culture that had been superimposed by the exchanges and negotiations of successive periods of struggle. What differentiated the earlier period from the later was the general belief in the former that the new capitalist industrial order was a temporary phenomenon soon to be radically changed. Some of the by-products of this mentality — elements of republicanism, secularism, popular self-education, cooperation, land reform, internationalism, etc., that had flourished in the pre-1850 period — lived on in diluted form, or on the fringes of Gladstonian liberalism. Stronger elements in the post-1870 period derived from forms of working-class organization which now accepted the capitalist social order as the inevitable framework of action for the foreseeable future (trades unions and their political counterpart the Labour Representation Committee, which evolved into the Labour Party). The Labour Party was the apotheosis of the 'now enclosed and defensive world of working class-culture', which not only accepted capitalism, but monarchy, Empire, aristocracy and established religion as well [14].

Although Gareth Stedman Jones writes in terms of a cultural process of 'making' and 'remaking' of the English working class, his discussion also suggests that some continuity exists as the result of the superimposition of new layers of culture. The working-class consciousness of the post-1870 period took on a more defensive character and accepted its location within a relatively settled social hierarchy, whereas in the earlier period it has been more radical and challenging. However, even with respect to this political aspect there remained traces of the earlier radicalism within the 'folk' memory of the working class, and these continued as a living presence that could make itself felt in periods of crisis and as part of the heritage of thinking on the Left in British politics. After all, it can be argued that the working-class political radicalism of Owenism and Chartism, like the middle-class liberalism, both had common roots in the older traditions of the Enlightenment such as the emphasis on the capacity of the individual for self-improvement and a reverence for reason. If working-class culture is considered more broadly than simply with respect to its political orientation, it is important not to push too far the notion of a rupture or 'remaking', with its misleading connotations of total transformation. Gareth Stedman Jones criticizes Richard Hoggart's book. *The Uses of Literacy* (1957) for describing the working-class culture of the North of England industrial towns in the 1930s as 'traditional', when in fact, according to Stedman Jones, it had its roots in the late nineteenth century, in the breakdown of an earlier, more separatist and politically orientated working-class culture. This criticism of Hoggart runs the risk of overstressing the political orientation of working-class culture as its defining characteristic and neglecting the continuities within its 'lived culture'. (The tendency is encouraged by the fact that Stedman Jones's study is based on evidence confined to the 'conditions of emergence of a new working-class culture in *London*', although some supportive evidence for its wider applicability is drawn from Hobsbawm's *Industry and Empire* (1968)).

It is true that Hoggart's study drew its evidence mainly from the skilled-working-class culture of Hunslet, which would be likely to reflect values of the post-1870 aristocracy of labour. Hoggart himself acknowledged this when he described the physical setting as late-Victorian and the buildings as having been there since 'about 1870'. However, he also referred to the capacity of the working-class culture 'not only to resist change but to assimilate, modify and adapt to traditional ends, things which looked at first like major agents of change' [15]. This view was echoed by Robert

Roberts's *The Classic Slum* (1973), which considered an older and more 'classic' working-class neighbourhood that had been described by Engels in the 1940s, and still had many longstanding cultural features continuing into the twentieth century. Roberts remarked on the complex and longstanding stratification of the working-class community, where even the unskilled workers 'split into plainly defined groups according to occupations, possessions and family connection', and below these he noted a 'series of castes, some unknown and others, it seems, already withered into insignificance in Professor Hoggart's Hunslet of the 1930s' [16].

Roberts, like Hoggart, chronicles the impact of new, mass-circulation literature and other commercial entertainments on the culture of the working class. But, as with Hoggart, he also mentioned some of the important oral traditions of that culture — proverbs and popular sayings, children's street-lore and singing games that had been passed on, with modifications, from generation to generation. It is to these and other elements and layers of working-class culture that I wish to turn next. They provide fascinating material for developing a sociological perspective on culture as multi-layered, sedimented, *and* negotiated (negotiated in an exchange between different sorts and sources of cultural input, as well as between different classes and social strata). There are a variety of methods for analysing culture viewed in this way, drawing on the disciplines of folklore, anthropology, and sociology. But there is also a sense in which, what is being recommended is akin to Foucault's approach of an 'archaeology' of knowledge and belief, although without being committed to his focus on 'regimes of truth', or 'epistemological breaks', concerned with codes of knowledge of 'discursive formations' such as medical, penological, or sexual discourses [17]. In so far as we are concerned with discourses and codes, it is with those that constitute popular culture rather than those which claim to establish expert knowledges (whilst accepting that popularized versions of expert knowledge do penetrate popular culture and can become one of its constituents).

LAYERS OF CULTURE

The notion of an archaeology of culture is useful in so far as it suggests that it is necessary to excavate different layers of culture, which are in a sense discontinuous. Cultural studies have frequently lapsed into a 'wholistic' and deductivist approach which views the parts of culture as explicable and decodable as parts of a whole, totality, or system. Find the principle that binds the whole, the code that unlocks the system, and the elements can be explained by deduction. This was the approach of Hegel, of some versions of Marxism, functionalism, and of all those whe set out to analyse cultures with a 'total history' approach. Foucault contrasted 'total history' with 'general history' and *The Archaeology of Knowledge* has been described as a study of the theoretical problems posed by the use in 'general history' of such concepts as discontinuity, rupture, threshold, limit, series and transformation. The difference between the two sorts of history is that:

'Total history' drew all phenomena around a single centre — the principle, meaning, spirit, world-view, overall form of a society or civilization. The same form of historicity operated on economic, social, political and religious beliefs and practices, subjecting them to the same type of transformation and dividing up the temporal succession of events into great periods, each possessing its own principle of cohesion. 'General history', on the other hand, speaks of 'series, segmentations, limits, differences of level, time-lags, anachronistic survivals, possible types of relation'. It is not simply a juxtaposition of different histories or series — economic, political, cultural, etc. — nor the search for analogies or coincidences between them. The task proposed by general history is to determine what forms of relations may legitimately be made between them. [18]

Marx launched one of the first attacks on total histories, such as Hegel's and their view of uninterrupted historical continuities centred on a 'Subject' founded on human consciousness. However, Foucault, like his former teacher Althusser, criticized the tendency of some Marxists to turn Marx into a historian of totality centring on a human Subject (the Proletariat as an agent with a purpose to fulfil in achieving the end of History). Foucault is interested in discerning how cultural formations ('discursive formations') of various types, such as nineteenth-century psychopathology, are made to appear rational and unified, he wishes to deconstruct them, and to show how a unifying object of discourse comes to be formed — what are the rules of its formation. In so doing, he produces fascinating insights into the articulation of different institutions, practices, and ways of thinking, in a particular period. Thus in the case of nineteenth-century psychopathology he shows how the term 'madness' came be applied to certain forms of behaviour, and how appropriate methods of control and treatment of that 'object' could be specified. He traced the emergence of this discursive formation across several social or cultural areas — the family, the immediate social group, the work situation, and the religious community. What he resists is the temptation to subsume these formative or constituting properties under a single causal or essential principle. It is for this reason that, in works like *The Birth of the Clinic* (1963/73), he rejects attempts to link the various discursive and non-discursive practices by reference to homologies or coincidences, or the Marxist alternative of explaining the discursive practices as being semi-autonomous but determined 'in the last instance' by the mode of production (e.g. as Althusser does). The value of Foucault's contribution does not lie in offering a theoretical resolution to the problem of finding *the* articulating principle of a cultural complex, or the final cause of its ideological effects. Its main value is in showing the fruitfulness of an archaeological method that drives us back again and again to uncovering the layers of culture, their specific interrelations, and the political processes (both micro- and macro-) that produce their ideological outcome (although Foucault resists references to ideology).

Culture has been conceptualized as layered in two senses — the diachronic and the synchronic. It is diachronically layered as the result of the superimposition of successive cultural productions over a period of time. The periods over which cultural practices emerge and then become crystallized and institutionalized vary in duration, from the *durée* of the passing moment (events) to the *longue durée* of 'deeply sediment time–space relations' as Giddens describes them (drawing on the historian Braudel's terms to describe his plottings of different time-spans from events to demographic and institutional trends, and beyond these to physical surroundings, in his history of the Mediterranean world) [19]. The synchronic relations between layers of culture refer to the articulation of different cultural elements, and includes consideration of their varying degrees of crystallization and institutionalization, ranging from the most fluid cultural forms to those that are enforced by institutionalized sanctions.

Georges Gurvitch, seeking to avoid the dangers of 'wholistic' approaches pointed out by Foucault (of assuming a homology between part and whole, or of integrating the part into the whole on the basis of a universal determining principle in the last instance), combined the diachronic and the synchronic in a sociology of 'depth levels'. Like Foucault, he emphasized discontinuties between different structural formations, and resisted the danger of 'abstract culturalism' inherent in structuralism; whilst structuralists drew their inspiration from structural linguistics, and spoke of the 'grammar' of culture, Gurvitch evoked the picture of structure as a 'balancing act' or precarious equilibrium, in a moving field of force and power. He visualized social life in two dimensions, analogous to a horizontal axis and a vertical axis which intersect. The vertical axis corresponds to the levels of depth ranked according to the degree to which cultural forms are crystallized, and the horizontal axis refers to those types of social frameworks in which these levels of depth are visible. Durkheim had recognized five such levels; at the deeper levels social life was relatively spontaneous and creative, while at its more visible, surface levels, it showed itself through quite regular and predictable patterns of behaviour, as follows:

1. The 'morphological' or surface level, consisting of the material and visible aspects of society; its geography and demography, and the products of human activity which are 'social' in so far as they are human creations and carry social meanings.
2. Social institutions, both in the sense of organizations and in the sense of regular patterns of behaviour.
3. Symbols, consisting of rituals and customs which, like flags, emblems and badges, serve as 'rallying-signs' for a group.
4. Collective ideas and values which provide the inspiration for institutionalization of social activity and which are summed up in symbols.
5. The collective consciousness itself, consisting of collective memories, feelings, aspirations, etc. [20].

Gurvitch developed these into ten depth-levels:

1. *The morphological and ecological surface.* This is social in that it is penetrated and transformed by human action, as in the case of those material objects that become 'property'.
2. *Social organizations.* These are pre-established collective patterns of behaviour that are regulated, ordered and centralized in a more or less rigid manner. They are one of the modes of social control, both over their participants and over the more spontaneous elements of social life.
3. *Social patterns or models.* These are the more or less standardized images of expected collective behaviour, the signs, signals and rules that give regularity to collective behaviour. They extend beyond particular domains of organizations and are more flexible; hence they constitute a depth level between organizations and collective behaviour extraneous to any organization. Both technical and aesthetic models are included in this category — from mundane aspects of daily life, such as cooking recipes, economic techniques, to models that reveal the character of the religion, art and education of the society. Collective signals and signs are a particular case of social models; they differ from symbols in that they express fairly completely whatever signification they are intended to convey, which is not the case with symbols. (The science of signs and signification, 'semiology', has

advanced a great deal since Gurvitch wrote, particularly through the work of figures such as Roland Barthes and Umberto Eco.)

4. *Regular collective behaviour not confined to social organizations.* This is subjacent to the social models and is expected to realize those models, but it often deviates from them to varying degree. This more or less regular behaviour is ranked by Gurvitch according to the amount of spontaneity it exhibits:

   (a) Ritual and procedural behaviour, based on rigorously regulated traditions, e.g. religious rites, judicial procedures.
   (b) Practices, mores, routines, folkways.
   (c) Fashions and fads.
   (d) Behaviour that is insubordinate and non-conformist in relation to the social models.

5. *The web of social roles.* These are more spontaneous and flexible complexes of behaviour than the previous levels because they depend so much more on individual creative performance. However, Gurvitch stressed that a role only exists as part of a social matrix, and the social drama of role performance involves groups and not just individuals.

6. *Collective attitudes.* This refers to shared dispositions and motivations to act in certain ways. Gurvitch warned against the distorted version of these produced by public opinion pollsters based on the faltering and artificially elicited answers to questions directed to the so-called 'average individual'.

7. *Social symbols.* These are extemely variable and pervasive, and they operate as a kind of social cement or communicative network. They are, however, always to some extent ambiguous, for a symbol never fully expresses the meaning which it is supposed to convey, and so can be interpreted in ways which may conflict, thereby promoting greater spontaneity than models.

8. *Spontaneous, innovative, and creative collective behaviour.* This is collective behaviour that not only stands outside the crystallized and standardized models and symbols, but also seeks to replace them. It changes the meanings of established models and symbols, and upsets their hierarchy. In periods of crisis, revolution, religious reformation, great reform, migrations, and discoveries, this kind of behaviour can play a decisive role.

9. *Collective ideas and values.* They provide the direction and orientation for all the more organized levels and which these only express in piecemeal fashion.

10. *Collective mentalities or collective consciousness.* They represent an

masses, and more varied than in communions. Conmunions depend on collective intuitions (in the phenomenological sense of that term, which distinguishes it from reflection and categorization), whereas masses manifest crude symbolic images. Communities are wider in their field of vision, and actualize a variety of mental states and mental acts, particularly those based on reflection, such as conceptualizations and judgements. Masses and communions are less stable and more short-lived than communities, and they appear sporadically; for example, large groups frequently display the mass form of sociality, especially when they lack contiguity (as is usually the case with social classes and publics), whilst religious sects, at least in their originating, evidence the sociality of communion. In periods of war and social crisis, however, global societies can proliferate communions and masses rather than communities. These differences have important implications for the assertion of cultural hegemony, or the development of ideological communities, whether of classes or nations, and for the mobilization of people to action.

The extent to which groups can become cultural communities determines their chances of resisting the penetration of the symbol systems, ideologies or discourses of otherwise dominant groups in a society. Theorists as politically opposed as the American functionalist Talcott Parsons, and the French Marxist Louis Althusser, have tended to exaggerate the extent to which the culture of politically and economically dominant social classes can penetrate and mobilize subordinate classes. As we have seen, critics of the dominant ideology thesis make the case that only dominant class groups have ever been strongly committed to dominant ideologies. This could be because, on several depth-levels of culture, below that of institutionalized disciplines, the subordinate classes constitute communities which contain elements that are resistant to penetration and mobilization. Giddens has suggested three forms of such resistance: divergent subcultures, subordinate groups' awareness or seeing-through of the social forms which oppress them, and cultural mechanisms of 'distancing' (such as working-class humour) [21]. I would like to turn to an examination of studies of some of these sources of resistance to penetration and ideological mobilization, drawn from various cultural depth-levels.

EPISTEMIC COMMUNITIES AND IDEOLOGICAL COMMUNITIES

Implicit in Gramsci's work, and more explicit in Gurvitch's *The Social Frameworks of Knowledge*, is an awareness of ways in which differences in the forms of knowledge which predominate in various communities present barriers or resistance to their assimilation into hegemonic ideological communities. It is a fact that the different conditions of life of various groups give rise to sub-cultures which differ in the bases of their knowledge; they form 'epistemic communities' which cannot be assimilated into 'ideological communities' without a great deal of struggle. The problem of penetration and assimilation of those epistemic communities presents a challenge to any group which seeks to recruit them to its cause, whether it is a revolutionary movement or a dominant bloc, such as management, Church leaders, or other institutional elites (including what Althusser calls Ideological State Apparatuses). Gramsci pointed out the challenge that this presents to attempts to impose a coherent philosophy/ideology on the masses, whether the attempt is by socialist philosophers or Catholic theologians. People are members of more than one group and because of this, and the disjointed nature of 'popular philosophy', their thinking is incoherent and episodic, containing 'stratified deposits' of past philosophies which leave in people 'an infinity of traces without an inventory'. Similarly, common-sense, which is the 'philosophy of non-philosophers', is the 'conception of the world which is uncritically absorbed by the various social and cultural environments in which the moral individuality of the average man is developed'. Gramsci describes it as the 'folklore' of philosophy, and like folklore 'it takes countless different forms'. Its most fundamental characteristic is that it is 'fragmentary, incoherent and inconsequential, in conformity with the position of those masses whose philosophy it is'. It is only on those occasions in history when a 'homogeneous social group is brought into being' that there emerges 'in opposition to common sense, a homogeneous — in other words coherent and systematic — philosophy'. Such coherent philosophies, if they are imposed from the outside on the masses of subordinate groups, as in the case of the great philosophical systems or the religion of Church leaders, have no direct influence on the people, according to Gramsci. What influence they have is not through ideological integration, 'winning hearts and minds', but 'as an external political force, an element of cohesive force exercised by the ruling classes and therefore an element of subordination to an external hegemony' [22].

The overall message of Gramsci's discussion of common-sense thinking, spontaneous philosophy of the masses, and popular religion, is that they are resistant to efforts to assimilate them into ideological communities that derive from the culture of the dominant classes or their intellectual strata. An institution such as the Catholic Church could attain only a surface unity:

Every religion, even Catholicism (indeed Catholicism more than any, precisely because of its efforts to retain a 'surface' unity and avoid splintering into national churches and social stratifications), is in reality a multiplicity of distinct and often contradictory religions: there is one Catholicism for the peasants, one for the petit-bourgeois and town workers, one for women, and one for intellectuals which is itself varegated and disconnected. But common sense is influenced not only by the crudest and least elaborated forms of these sundry Catholicisms as they exist today. Previous religions have also had an influence and remain components of common sense to this day, and the same is true of previous forms of present Catholicism — popular heretical movements, scientific superstitions connected with past cults, etc. In common sense it is the 'realistic', materialist elements which are predominant, the immediate product of crude sensation. This is by no means in contradistinction with the religious element, far from it. But here these elements are 'superstitions' and acritical. [23]

We have already referred to this contrast between popular religion and official religion and simply note at this stage that Gramsci's depiction of it is supported by many studies by sociologists of religion, from Max Weber to William Christian's *Person and God in a Spanish Valley* (1974) [24]. Christian (*sic*), in his description of the religious life of Catholics in the Nansa Valley of Northern Spain in the 1960s, described the co-existence of three levels of religion even within a relatively homogeneous community. The oldest layer probably antedates Christianity and manifests itself in the shrines which influence specific areas, such as province, valley or village, and corresponds to the local sense of identity. These shrines also help to deal with concrete problems: soliciting divine energy for human purpose and eliciting human energy for divine purposes. The next layer, deriving from the impulses of the Counter-Reformation, is characterized by a sense of sin and fear of purgatory and includes general devotions, such as the Sacred Heart and the Rosary, whose objective is personal salvation and the transmission of persons from one spiritual condition to another. The latest layer, the product of new intellectual trends, derived from the initiative of young priests attempting to instill a theology which taught people to find God in one another rather than through intermediaries. The various layers are relatively discontinuous and incoherent, despite the efforts of a professional intellectual group, the clergy, to produce an integrated and coherent symbol system.

If there is even discontinuity and incoherence at the symbolic level, it is not surprising that there are difficulties at the epistemic level. Some writers on ideology, such as Clifford Geertz, have greatly illuminated ideological processes at the level of symbol systems, but neglected to consider the other levels listed by Gurvitch [25]. Giddens has pointed out that the most 'buried' forms of ideology 'are likely to be deeply sedimented in both a psychological and an historical sense'. He draws on Norbert Elias's studies of the 'civilizing process' over very long periods of time to make the point that the repressions sustaining 'privacy' and 'self-discipline' in day-to-day life are part of the post-feudal 'civilizing process' which proceeds through the increasing confinement or 'hiding behind the scenes' of that which is distasteful, particularly certain body functions [26]. Such practices are highly crystallized patterns of behaviour, in Gurvitch's depth-level terms, but are unconsciously routinized, and vary between different communities.

Similarly, whereas Parsonian functionalism emphasizes the ideological integration performed at the level of collective values, and the importance of the internationalization of values as motivational components of personality, it can be argued that some of what Giddens call 'the most deeply sedimented elements of social conduct' are epistemic, or cognitively established. For example, the reproduction of language is not a motivated phenomenon, although speech acts are not unrelated to the wants of a speaker. Yet the mutual intelligibility of acts and of discourse, achieved in and through language, is perhaps the most basic condition of sustained interaction or community [27]. Routine actions are saturated by the taken-for-granted; that is to say, the knowledge which members of that community have about what is required to perform such actions correctly, is largely 'unconscious' — it depends on 'ethno-methods'. The nuances of ethno-methods, of routines, and language use, vary from one social framework to another, and produce barriers and distances that make them resistant to an imposed ideological hegemony. Gramsci's conception of common sense was relatively undifferentiated. He frequently referred to folklore and popular religion as examples of it, and viewed these as resistant to, or contestative of, official conceptions of the world. Gurvitch, by contrast, went to great lengths to differentiate these various depth-levels of culture, and to delineate different types of knowledge, which he then suggested would appear in a particular hierarchy of importance for each social framework (forms of sociality — mass, community, communion; types of groups, including classes; societies). Some of these distinctions are potentially very important for the study of ideology. For example, Gurvitch's list of types of knowledge included perceptual knowledge of the external world (involving different perceptions of time and space, a factor that has been emphasized recently by Giddens in his theory of structuration); knowledge of the Other and the We; common-sense knowledge;

technical knowledge; political knowledge; scientific knowledge; philosophical knowledge. He discussed the ways in which the character of these and their hierarchy of importance varies as between classes such as peasants, the proletariat, and the bourgeoisie (he also considered the evidence for an incipient 'techno-bureaucratic class'). What emerges from these discussions is the possibility that each of these classes may present different sorts of resistance and receptiveness to ideological assimilation, and on different cultural levels. This presents a way of theoretically integrating the three sorts of resistance listed by Giddens: resistance as a result of divergent sub-culture; subordinate groups awareness or seeing-through of the social forms which oppress them; and the cultural mechanisms of 'distancing' (such as working class humour). Successful resistance through one or more of these mechanisms, which we will now discuss further, could explain why ideological penetration or assimilation of subordinate groups is only sporadic or superficial. This seems a potentially more fruitful line of enquiry than that which poses the question of ideology in terms of explaining a non-event — the non-appearance or inadequate development of a revolutionary class consciousness (the problematic of a 'total history' version of Marxism). It still allows us to ask questions about why the extension and maintenance of an ideological community at the societal level is often restricted, and why nationalisms, society-wide dominant ideologies, or even a proletarian class-for-itself, may only appear as brief 'communions' in periods of crisis and fail to sustain themselves as ideological communities. (It should be borne in mind that we are now considering the question of how social order and social reproduction may rest on 'consent', even if it is only the tacit consent to routine; this is different from the question of how institutionalized social disciplines coerce compliance).

FOLK-CULTURE, SUB-CULTURE, AND RESISTANCE

The 1970s saw a revival in Britain of studies of sub-cultures, viewed as sources of resistance to a dominant class culture. Some of the best studies were concerned with youth sub-cultures and emanated from the Centre for Contemporary Cultural Studies at Birmingham, as in the collection edited by Stuart Hall and Tony Jefferson, *Resistance Through Rituals: Youth sub-cultures in post-war Britain* (1977), and in books by two of the contributors, Dick Hebdige, *Subculture: The Meaning of Style* (1979), and Paul Willis, *Learning to Labour* (1977) [28]. These were highly original works and drew on theoretical sources new to this field, particularly those derived from Gramsci and Althusser, and they examined sub-cultures in terms of resistance to hegemonic domination. They were characterized by an effort to avoid seeing sub-cultures not just as ideological constructs — imaginary resolutions to real problems — but also in terms of whether they won space for the subordinate groups and kept hegemonic domination at a distance.

Although the theoretical framework was different, these studies represented a revival of interest in an old topic which had fascinated students of folklore, from the early years of the disciplines of sociology and antropology in Britain, to Gramsci and his successors who studied folklore in Italy. The topic was the resistance, presented by the very existence of sub-cultures, to an official culture that sought to dominate thought, to lay down the terms defining what made sense, and which castigated such sub-cultures as 'superstition', 'deviant', 'irrational', and 'obstacles to progress' or modernization, etc. Some Italian folklorists, such as Lombardi-Satriani, have followed Gramsci's lead in viewing folklore as inherently contestative of the culture of the dominant class. Lombardi-Satriani quotes with approval Gramsci's statement that folklore should be studied

> as a 'concept of the world and of life' implying in a large measure definite strata (set in time and space) of society, in contraposition (that, too, being for the most part inherent, mechanical and objective) to the 'official' conceptions of the world (or in a larger sense, of the cultured parts of society as historically determined) which have happened through history. [29]

This Gramscian view of folklore has been criticized by some folklorists for portraying a rather mechanical and static contraposition of two cultures, the subordinate and the 'official'. He seemed to be suggesting that the subordinate culture automatically contests the dominant official culture simply by being there, i.e. it is contestative implicitly by virtue of its position. Lombardi-Satriani defends this on the grounds that Gramsci's interpretation does explain the characteristic resistance that the masses have put up against the attempt of the organized powers of the official institutions (especially the Church) to absorb them into its culture. According to Lombardi-Satriani, the cultural resistance of the subordinate class to absorption by the dominant culture has the value of 'adducing other testimony' contraposed to the self-proclaimed universality of the cultural forms of the class in power. The most useful contribution that Gramsci made to folklore studies was to dispel the idea that folklore consisted solely of cultural 'fossils' and survivals, and he did this by indentifying folklore as part of the cultural complex lying outside the institutionalized norms and official conceptions propagated by the organized sectors of society. To what extent such elements of 'unofficial' culture are contestative is a matter for empirical investigation in each case. However, this conception does focus on the potentiality for resistance and contestation that is inherent in sub-cultures.

The use of the term 'sub-culture', in studies of youth sub-cultures and industrial sub-cultures, echoes the conception of culture as stratified and layered that was prevalent among the first generation of professional sociologists, anthropologists and folklorists in Britain. There are at least three possible connotations of the prefix in the word *sub*-culture: (i) part of a larger whole; (ii) subordination; (iii) 'beneath the surface'. The first meaning is common within functionalist sociology, where it implies that even 'deviant' sub-cultures exist within a more fundamental cultural unity. It is also present in the Marxist studies of youth sub-cultures which make reference to a 'double articulation' of youth sub-cultures — first to their 'parent' culture (e.g. working-class culture), second, to the dominant culture. The second meaning, that of subordination, directs attention to the existence of potential conflict, as in those aspects of the studies of youth sub-cultures which portray them as styles of resistance to hegemony. The third meaning, with its connotation of 'beneath the surface', suggests that culture might be conceptualized as 'layered'. This conception exists within the Gramscian theoretical framework of the Birmingham CCCS studies, which maintain that both the dominant culture and the subordinate cultures are layered:

> The dominant culture of a complex society is never a homo-geneous structure. It is layered, reflecting different interests within the dominant class (e.g. an aristocratic versus a bourgeois outlook), containing different traces from the past (e.g. religious ideas within a largely secular culture), as well as emergent elements in the present. Subordinate cultures will not always be in open conflict with it. They may, for long periods, coexist with it, negotiate the spaces and gaps in it, make inroads into it 'warrening it from within'. [30]

It was the conception of culture as layered that excited fierce debate among British sociologists, anthropologists and folklorists in the early part of the twentieth century [31]. The question was whether the layers of culture were chronologicaly determined, in the sense that the surface layers were the most recent and corresponded to modern, scientific rationality, whereas the deeper layers were more primitive and concrete rather than abstract. Those who adopted the geological analogy tended to relegate folklore and many other 'sub-cultural' elements to the status of 'fossils' and 'survivals', doomed to be swept away by the spread of institutionalized rationality. In Britain the discipline of Folklore became identified with antiquarianism or, where it adopted a theoretical stance, with social evolutionism. For this reason and others, such as the development of sociology and anthropology as separate disciplines, the concentration of antropology on the colonies rather than on the ethnology of the home country, and the subsequent dependence of folklore on a vanishing race of gentlemen and lady amateur collectors, this approach fell into disrepute after the First World War. Since then there have been only brief revivals of interest in folklore or similar sub-cultural elements, as in the *Mass Observation* studies begun by Tom Harrisson in the 1930s, the work of Peter and Iona Opie on children's lore, and the research of Donald McKelvie and others on oral tradition and belief in northern working-class areas [32]. Until the upsurge of interest in youth sub-cultures, analysis of 'lived cultures' or 'every-day culture' tended to be rather limited in terms of its analytical techniques and theory. There were plenty of sociological studies of class communities and occupational communities, but they did not attempt cultural analysis on many 'depth-levels' and with respect to different styles and genres, nor did they locate these within a theoretical framework of active cultural resistance to hegemony.

The new studies of youth sub-cultures were able to combine their Gramascian theoretical framework with techniques of cultural analysis drawn from French structuralists, such as Claude Lévi-Strauss and Roland Barthes, particularly in analysing sub-cultural 'styles'. The combination is most effective in Hebdige's discussion of resistance through style. Hebdige shows that the tension between dominant and subordinate groups can be found reflected in the surface levels of sub-culture, in styles composed of mundane objects which have a double meaning. He is clearly inspired by Roland Barthes' use of models derived from Saussure's linguistics. Barthes, in *Mythologies* (1957/72), sought to expose the normally hidden set of rules, codes and conventions through which meanings particular to specific social groups (the dominant ones) are 'naturalized' — rendered universal and 'given' for the whole society [33]. Hebdige, in his study of the styles of various youth sub-cultures — mods and rockers, skinheads and punks, rastas, etc. — combines Barthes' analytical techniques with Althusser's emphasis on ideology as inscribed in practices, and Gramsci's view of hegemony as a moving equilibrium of relations between classes and class fractions. His work was representative of the new upsurge of interest in the capacity of sub-cultures to disclose and challenge the real and hidden structures of dominance that lie beneath the surface of a seemingly natural and rational culture.

These studies of youth sub-cultures also reveal some of the limitations of style as a strategy of resistance to hegemonic culture, at least in so far as the concept of style is confined to the leisure field and is not applied to sub-cultural styles *within* major institutions. John Clarke pointed out that the limitation of these stylistic rebellions derived in part from the fact that they were simply an intensified adoption of that aspect of their working-class parents' culture which saw leisure as a significant area of 'relative class freedom':

> By posing their 'solutions' within this arena alone, the subcultural movements make a 'magical' attempt at resolving the contradictions which face them, for the displacement to leisure involves the *suppression* rather than the transcendence of those other key areas where the contradictions are generated. The suppression takes the form of a purely magical transcendence of work and family. [34]

Youth sub-cultures with a leisure focus were able to insert themselves at the transitional weak point in the chain of socialization between the family/school nexus and integration into the work process. When they took on family and work responsibilities, the youths found themselves subjected to the regulatory disciplines of those institutions, and their previous attachment to a sub-cultural leisure style declined. (Clarke suggests that middle-class hippies had relatively more space to generate alternative strategies for work, family and sexuality, and so the 'hippie career' lasted longer) [35]. Within the work-place it was adult working-class culture that supplied most of the elements that constituted the sub-culture relative to the hegemony of the official organizational culture.

According to Willis, boys come to consent to their future as labourers because such work is associated with the cultural apprenticeship they receive which stresses the masculinity of hard work and 'really doing things'. However, this does not preclude resistance, as the masculine ethos also resents authority and control. The masculine shop-floor sub-culture distanced itself from the hegemonic demands of the organization by a distinctive form of language and a highly developed humour. Willis found that up to half the verbal exchanges were not serious or about work activities. They were jokes that were vigorous, sharp, sometimes cruel, and often hinged around prime tenets of the culture such as disruption of production or subversion of the bosses' authority and status. Willis tended to contrast only two work-place cultures — the masculine working-class sub-culture and the official organizational culture, which he equated with middle-class culture. However, there are many other work sub-cultures. Pollert has used Willis's study of the process by which working-class boys slot themselves into manual work as a point of comparison to the socialization of girls [36]. In contrast to the boys, girls — particularly working-class — are groomed for marriage. Pollert found that the girls in her case study were aware of the futility of their work, but as it was not their primary interest, the resulting low commitment could easily be translated into stoical acceptance of the organization of production. Furthermore, the feminine culture of escape and romance, with its stress on individualism and competitiveness, acted to defuse conflict, even allowing for its parallel function as a shared set of meanings impenetrable to the work of management and men.

Perhaps the best example of the microsocial processes by which a work group can develop its own sub-culture, which distances if from the official organization culture, was provided by Donald Roy's study, 'Banana Time, Job Satisfaction and Informal Interaction' [37]. Roy's study is fascinating not so much as an example of informal work-group resistance, but for its phenomenological analysis of the various depth-levels of the group sub-culture, such as its construction and perception of space and time. Within the limits set by the demands of the production process, the work group constructed its own little world, which revolved around rituals such as banana time, peach time, opening the window time, coke time, and so on. Ritualized horseplay, as in Willis's study, was prominent: every day, for example, one worker would bring in a banana for a snack, and every day the others would sneak it away, eat it, and taunt him. These sub-cultural practices and perceptions may seem trivial and absurd, but they were performed in the face of managerial disapproval of horseplay and the other distractions that the managers viewed as frivolous and time-wasting. The official organizational culture imposed discipline, but consent to its hegemonic leadership was kept to a minimum by the impenetrability of the dense sub-culture of the work group.

The ideological effects of the various elements of lived cultures can only be fully appreciated by the adoption of something like an archaeological approach to uncovering the depth-levels or layers of culture. One important methodological reason for recommending this approach is that it can disclose discontinuities between these layers, and their ideological effects, and so prevent us from assuming that they are necessarily cumulative or parts of a unified whole. This synchronic discontinuity has its parallel in the historical dimension with respect to periodization. Hence, whether and to what extent hegemony is achieved by the dominant class in a specific period is a matter for investigation. The use of the term hegemony to suggest the unending and unproblematic exercise of class power, and the complete incorporation of the subordinate classes into the dominant class culture, sacrifices the capacity for historical specificity that the concept possessed in Gramsci's usage. For Gramsci, as we have noted, hegemony referred to a 'moving equilibrium', containing 'relations of forces favourable or unfavourable to this or that tendency'. The character and content of the balance struck between these contending forces can only be established by looking at concrete situations at specific historical moments. This view of structuration, in terms of a moving equilibrium, is very similar to Gurvitch's, and directs attention to the forces of restructuration and destructuration inherent in the cultural components of society [38].

IN CONCLUSION: WHAT DO PEOPLE BELIEVE?

Most of this book has been concerned with specifying the different levels of culture and the various ways in which they can have ideological effects. We have emphasized that these ideological effects can be achieved (and resisted) at a variety of levels, including the deeply sedimented attitudes and routines of daily life, the shifting significations of language, institutionalized disciplines, powerful symbols, intellectual doctrines and philosophies, and so on. And yet, there is still the temptation to ask impatiently: But what do people really believe? Certainly the public-opinion pollsters continue to make a living by supplying one sort of answer to that question. However, without going into the methodological problems of these surveys of beliefs or attitudes, it should be obvious by now that the answers they give are at best superficial, and at their worst, seriously misleading and even manipulative.

How much can we know about what ordinary people (as distinct from 'intellectuals') really believe? Rodney Needham claims to have experienced dizziness when writing his *Belief, Language and Experience* (1972) as a result of trying to answer the question. He added a warning to ethnographers that 'people do not necessarily believe what their culture trains them to say' [39]. Needham's concern was with the problem of understanding other cultures, but his arguments apply just as much to the problems and dangers involved in studying our fellow citizens. As Robert Towler puts it:

We are aware that not all Americans believe the same things, and that not all Britons believe the same things; we must become alert to the fact that not all Americans mean the same thing when they say that they 'believe' something, and that Britons are in the same predicament. Two professional philosophers, one a member of the Plymouth Brethren and the other a member of the Divine Light Mission, will be able to discuss 'belief' by drawing on a received philosophy of mind which they share as professional philosophers, but they will employ the word differently when they are in their respective sectarian milieux. [40]

Towler discusses the limitations of the method of questionnaire surveys as a way of discerning what people believe, and in his research on the thousands of letters received by the Bishop of Woolwich about the controversial theological book, *Honest to God*, he employs the methods of content analysis in order to develop a typology of conventional religious-ness [41]. However, even here there are problems, for the result of such methods tell us only a limited amount about what people believe, as they are themselves a response to intellectualized doctrinal statements. We are back at our starting point of the problem which theorists of ideology have had in deciding whether to adopt a narrow definition of ideology, which confines it to fairly clearly-defined belief-systems, or whether it is prefer-able to look at as many levels of culture as possible with the aim of discerning to what extent they combine to have an ideological effect. There is room for both approaches, indeed the second can include the first, whilst pointing out the implications of concentrating on only a limited range of cultural levels. One of those implications, for an area such as the sociology of religion, is that it can become one-sidedly concerned with the subjecti-vity of the social actor, as manifested in the analysis of religious belief systems, world-views, definitions of alternative realities, commitments to the sacred cosmos and so forth, which have dominated the sociology of religion since the success of Peter Berger's *The Social Reality of Religion* (1969). To paraphrase Bryan Turner: the question 'What is religion/ ideology, from the subjective perspective of the social actor?' has replaced the question 'What are the social/ideological effects of religious pheno-mena in society?' Furthermore, because subjectively has been examined at the level of belief-systems, largely formulated and articulated by intellec-tuals, there has been a tendency to assume that the 'social presence of beliefs was evidence that such beliefs have direct and specific social consequences' and that their presence was evidence of incorporation into a dominant ideology [42]. The discussion in this book can be read in part as a response to Turner's observation that the sociology of religion has fallen into the position of a 'theoretical side-show' as a result of its neglect of neo-Marxist debates about ideology, French structuralist discussions of subjectivity and power, and critical theory's discussion of knowledge, the state and legitimacy. We have not addressed all these issues, and the topics covered have not been confined to religion, but the challenge has been accepted.

REFERENCES

[1] N. Abercrombie, S. Hill and B. S. Turner, *The Dominant Ideology Thesis*, London, Allen & Unwin, 1980, p. 137.

[2] A. Gramsci, *Selections from the Prison Notebooks*, London, Lawrence & Wishart, 1971, p. 328.

[3] Chantal Mouffe, 'Hegemony and Ideology in Gramsci's, in Tony Bennett, G. Martin, C. Mercer and J. Woolacott (eds.), *Culture, Ideology and Social Process*. London, Batsford, 1981, 219–34, p. 231.

[4] A. Gramsci, *Quaderni dal Carcere*, ed. V. Gerratana, Turin, Einaudi, 1975, vol. 2, p. 1084, and quoted in Mouffe, op. cit., p. 232.

[5] Cf. Bernard Waites, Tony Bennett and Graham Martin (eds.), *Popular Culture: Past and Present*, London, Croom Helm, 1982, p. 17; and Tony Bennett, 'Popular Culture: themes and issues (2)', Unit 3 in Open University course *Popular Culture*, Milton Keynes, Open University Press, 1981, p. 7.

[6] Robert Gray, 'Bourgeois Hegemony in Victorian Britain', T. Bennett *et al.*, *Culture, Ideology and Social Process*, op. cit., pp. 235–249.

[7] Ibid., pp. 244–245.

[8] Ibid., p. 249, quoting a phrase used by Poulantzas.

[9] L. Senelick, 'Politics as Entertainment: Vistorian music-hall songs', in *Victorian Studies*, XIX, 1974. See the discussion by Bernard Waites, 'The Music Hall', Unit 5 in the Open University course *Popular Culture*, op. cit., p. 74.

[10] Cf. C. MacInnes, *Sweet Saturday Night*, London, MacGibbon & Kee, 1967, and Waites, op. cit.

[11] Waites, op. cit., pp. 74–75.

[12] Hugh Cunningham, *Leisure in the Industrial Revolution*, London, Vroom Helm, 1980; and also the excerpt 'Class and Leisure in Mid-Victorian England', in Waites, Bennett and Martin (eds.), op. cit., pp. 66–91.

[13] Gareth Stedman Jones, 'Working-class Culture and Working-class Politics in London, 1870–1900: Notes on the Remaking of a Working-class', in Waites, Bennett and Martin (eds.), op. cit., 92–121, pp. 116–117.

[14] Ibid., p. 118.
[15] Richard Hoggart, 'Changes in Working Class Life', in his *Speaking to Each Other*, Harmondsworth, Penguin, 1970, pp. 46 and 50. This essay provides some interesting reflections on the earlier work, *The Uses of Literacy*, Harmondsworth, Penguin, 1957. Cf., for what is regarded by Stedman Jones as a pioneer historical explanation of the origins of this culture, Eric Hobsbawm's *Industry and Empire*, London, 1968, pp. 135–137.
[16] Robert Roberts, *The Classic Slum*, Harmondsworth, Penguin, 1973, p. 21.
[17] Cf. Michel Foucault, *The Archaeology of Knowledge*, London, Tavistock, 1972; also the list of Foucault's works in Chapter 3, reference [44], above.
[18] Alan Sheridan, *Michel Foucault: The Will to Truth*, London, Tavistock, 1980, p. 92.
[19] Anthony Giddens, *Central Problems in Social Theory*, London, Macmillan, 1979, p. 110; and F. Braudel, *The Mediterranean and the Mediterranean World in the Age of Philip II*, 2 vols., London, 1972–73.
[20] Cf. the discussion of this Durkheimian model in K. Thompson, *Emile Durkheim*, London, Tavistock and Ellis Horwood, New York, Methuen, 1982, and its development and adaptation by Georges Gurvitch in *The Social Frameworks of Knowledge*, trans. by M. A. and K. A. Thompson, Blackwell, 1971, with an explanation of the links in my 'Introductory Essay', pp. ix–xxxviii. The following discussion of Gurvitch's model draws on that essay.
[21] Giddens, *Central Problems in Social Theory*, op. cit., p. 72.
[22] The quotations are from A. Gramsci, *Selections from the Prison Notebooks*, London, Lawrence & Wishart, 1971, pp. 324 and 419–420.
[23] Ibid., pp. 419–420.
[24] W. Christian, *Person and God in a Spanish Valley*, New York, Seminar Press, 1974.
[25] Clifford Geertz, 'Religion as a Cultural System', in M. Banton (ed.), *Anthropological Approaches to Religion*, London, Tavistock, pp. 1–46; and 'Ideology as a Cultural System', in D. Apter (ed.), *Ideology and Discontent*, New York, Free Press, pp. 47–76.
[26] Giddens, 1979, op. cit., p. 192, and Norbert Elias, *The Civilising Process*. Oxford, Blackwell, 1978.
[27] Giddens, 1979, op. cit., p. 218.
[28] Stuart Hall and Tony Jefferson, *Resistance through Rituals: Youth Subcultures in Post-war Britain*, London, Hutchinson, 1976; Dick

Hebdige, *Subculture: The Meaning of Style*, London, Methuen, 1979; Paul Willis, *Learning to Labour*, London, Saxon House, 1977.

[29] A. Gramsci, *Letteratura e vita nazionale*, Torino, 1954, p. 72, quoted in Luigi Lombardi-Satriani, 'Folklore as Culture of Contestation', in *Journal of the Folklore Institute* (Indiana), **XI**, 1/2 (June–August), 1974, 99–121, p. 105. Cf. the discussion of this in Kenneth Thompson, 'Folklore and Sociology', *The Sociological Review*, **28**, 2, May 1980, pp. 249–275.

[30] John Clarke *et al.*, 'Subcultures, Cultures and Class', in Hall and Jefferson (eds.), op. cit., 9–79, p. 12.

[31] Cf. the account in K. Thompson, 1980, op. cit.

[32] Cf. the Mass Observation study, *Britain*, Harmondsworth, Penguin, 1938; Peter and Iona Opie, *The Lore and Language of Schoolchildren*, Oxford, The Clarendon Press, 1959; Donald McKelvie, 'Aspects of Oral Tradition and Belief in an Industrial Region', *Folklife*, **1**, 1963, pp. 77–94, and 'Proverbial Elements in Oral Tradition of an English Urban Industrial Region', *Journal of the Folklore Institute*, **2**, 3, 1965, pp. 244–261.

[33] Roland Barthes, *Mythologies*, Paris, 1957, London, Cape, 1972.

[34] John Clarke, 'Style', in Hall and Jefferson (eds.), op. cit., 175–191, p. 189.

[35] Clarke, op. cit., p. 191.

[36] A. Pollert, *Girls, Wives, Factory Lives*, London, Macmillan, 1981.

[37] Donald Roy, 'Banana Time, Job Satisfaction and Informal Interaction', *Human Organization*, **18**, 1960, pp. 156–168; and in Graeme Salaman and Kenneth Thompson (eds.), *People and Organizations*, London, Longman, 1973.

[38] I do not accept Anthony Giddens's judgement that there is no room for a concept of destructuration such as that suggested by Gurvitch and that 'a notion of destructuration is only necessary if we retain the idea that structure is simply equivalent to constraint, thereby counterposing structure and freedom (as Gurvitch does and as Sarte does also).' (Giddens, 1979, op. cit., p. 70). I have explained that Gurvitch's concept of structuration is concerned with crystallization and patterning of elements, and that because the hierarchy of elements usually rests on a precarious equilibrium it is constantly vulnerable to destructuration and restructuration.

[39] Rodney Needham, *Belief, Language and Experience*, Oxford, Blackwell, 1972, p. 5.

[40] Robert Towler, *The Need for Certainty: A Sociological Study of Conventional Religion*, London, Routledge & Kegan Paul, 1984, p. 31.

[41] I am undertaking a similar analysis of the thousands of letters received by the Bishop of Durham in response to his controversial statements on the 1984–85 miners strike, and on other political and doctrinal issues.
[42] Bryan S. Turner, *Religion and Social Theory*, London, Heinemann Education (now Gower), 1983, pp. 4–5.

Recommended Reading

The following list is not intended to provide complete coverage of important works in the field. It offers some guidance to readers on where they can find fuller statements of the main issues that enter into the arguments put forward in this book. Readers should consult the references at the end of each chapter for more detailed sources of the data and arguments. Similarly, the works of classical social theorists are not listed here, although they are sometimes included in chapter references and there are selected extracts in some of the recommended books.

Nicholas Abercrombie, Stephen Hill and Bryan S. Turner, *The Dominant Ideology Thesis*, London, Allen & Unwin, 1980.

Veronica Beechey and James Donald (eds.), *Subjectivity and Social Relations*, Milton Keynes, Open University Press, 1985.

Robert Bocock and Kenneth Thompson (eds.), *Religion and Ideology*, Manchester, Manchester University Press, 1985.

Centre for Contemporary Cultural Studies (Birmingham), *On Ideology*, London, Hutchinson, 1978.

James Donald and Stuart Hall (eds.), *Politics and Ideology*, Milton Keynes, Open University Press, 1985.

Anthony Giddens, *Central Problems in Social Theory*, London, Macmillan, 1979.

Georges Gurvitch, *The Social Frameworks of Knowledge*, trans. by M. A. and K. A. Thompson, with an Introductory Essay by Kenneth Thompson, Oxford, Blackwell, and New York, Harper Torchbooks, 1971.

Jorge Larrain, *The Concept of Ideology*, London, Hutchinson, 1979.

Göran Therborn, *The Ideology of Power and the Power of Ideology*, London, New Left Books, 1980.

Kenneth Thompson, *Emile Durkheim*, London, Tavistock and Ellis Horwood, New York, Methuen, 1982.

Bryan S. Turner, *Religion and Social Theory*, London, Heinemann, 1983.

There are three articles that are particularly significant for the theoretical approach favoured in this book. They are: Stuart Hall, 'Signification, Representation, Ideology: Althusser and the Post-Structuralist Debates', in *Critical Studies in Mass Communication*, 2, 2, June 1985, pp. 91–114; Bernard Lacroix, '*The Elementary Forms of Religious Life* as a Reflection on Power (*Object Pouvoir*)', in *Critique of Anthropology*, 4, 13–14, 1979, pp. 87–103; Sheelagh Stawbridge, 'Althusser's Theory of Ideology and Durkheim's Account of Religion: An Examination of some Striking Parallels', in *Sociological Review*, 30, 1, 1982, pp. 125–140.

In addition to the above works, which are relevant to all the chapters in this book, there are certain major modern theorists whose writings are discussed in several chapters — such as Althusser, Foucault, Gramsci and Habermas. The references for these appear in those chapters.

There are several works that are relevant to particular topics but which can also be highly recommended for their more general qualities. Benedict Anderson provides a theoretically sophisticated and wide-ranging discussion of nationalism in his *Imagined Communities*, London, Verso, 1983. There are revealing historical accounts of the invention of national traditions in E. Hobsbawm and T. Ranger (eds.), *The Invention of Tradition*, Cambridge University Press, 1983. The relation of ideology to sub-cultures is illuminated by a number of publications from the Centre for Contemporary Cultural Studies, Birmingham, such as Stuart Hall and Tony Jefferson (eds.), *Resistance Through Rituals*, London, Hutchinson, 1976. The Open University's multi-media course on 'Popular Culture' was produced on the basis of collaboration between several disciplines and has a great deal of valuable teaching material that is relevant to the study of beliefs and ideology. The scope and approach of the course is revealed in two anthologies: B. Waites, T. Bennett and G. Martin (eds.), *Popular Culture: Past and Present*, London, Croom Helm, 1982; and T. Bennett, G. Martin, C. Mercer and J. Woollacott (eds.), *Culture, Ideology and Social Process*, London, Batsford, 1981.

Finally, although this book has put forward an approach towards beliefs and ideologies that is much broader than that of the sociology of religion, readers who wish to pursue that aspect concerned with the issue of 'secularization' should consult the following works: Alasdair MacIntyre, *Secularization and Moral Change*, Oxford University Press, 1967; David Martin, *A General Theory of Secularization*, Oxford, Blackwell, 1978; Bryan R. Wilson, *Contemporary Transformations of Religion*, Oxford University Press, 1976.

Index